Run Your Race

Reflections of My Life, My Love, and My Lord

Linda Hall Blacksmith

Run Your Race

Reflections of My Life, My Love, and My Lord

Trilogy Christian Publishers

A Wholly Owned Subsidiary of Trinity Broadcasting Network

2442 Michelle Drive

Tustin, CA 92780

For information, address Trilogy Christian Publishing

Rights Department, 2442 Michelle Drive, Tustin, Ca 92780.

Trilogy Christian Publishing/ TBN and colophon are trademarks of Trinity Broadcasting Network.

For information about special discounts for bulk purchases, please contact Trilogy Christian Publishing.

Manufactured in the United States of America

10 9 8 7 6 5 4 3 2 1

Library of Congress Cataloging-in-Publication Data is available.

ISBN 978-1-64773-269-1

ISBN 978-1-64773-270-7 (ebook)

To Bill Blacksmith, my husband of fifty-four years, the love of my life, my ministry partner, my best friend, and my soul mate. Life with you was a wonderful adventure.

To my children and grandchildren, who have contributed much to my contentment and healing during this time of change in my life. You all are great encouragers and know how to make me smile.

To my friends and extended family who have not missed a beat in care, support, and love toward me. You are all very special.

To my Lord Jesus Christ. With You my life has hope, peace, and joy.

CONTENTS

Acknowledgments 11

Introduction 13

Crossing the Finish Line 17

For All the Saints... 21

From Wailing to Dancing.. 23

Empty Closets and Memory Quilts 27

The Mashed Potato Disaster................................... 31

Where Are the Mousetraps? 35

This Is the Day... 39

Adventure Was His Middle Name 41

Save the Pie!.. 45

No Waves Allowed 49

For an Audience of One 53

Pom Poms and Megaphones................................... 57

A Prophetic Utterance 61

Wrestling with Love 63

Pool Balls a-Flying... 67

It Was Supposed to Bounce! 69

Macaroni Salad.. 73

Drive Up Along the Sidewalk 75

Camp Soles 79

Lord, Hear My Prayer 83

Thy Word Is a Lamp... 87

What Fills Your Heart? 91

Our Family.. 95

A Wrestling Champion 97

Various Trials 101

Bethel Covenant Community 105

West Virginia University 109

Sharing the Good News... 113

There's No Retirement in the Kingdom.......................... 117

It's All Greek to Me.. 121

Team Ministry... 123

The Wisdom of Rocky... 127

Worship and Service 129

What's the "Therefore" There For? 131

Thy Word Have I Hid in My Heart............................... 133

The Days of Dialysis... 137

The Halverson Benediction 141

Robe of Righteousness... 143

You've Got to Think Quickly on Your Feet 147

Egg Timer and Three Chapters 151

Whose Pager Is Beeping?.. 155

Life with a New Kidney 159

All Ideas Are Not Created Equal 163

What I Appreciate About You 167

Riviera Maya 169

We Need a Translator! 173

My Own Personal Missionary.. 177

The Train.. 181

Satisfying Desires at a Lower Level............................... 185

Words Do Matter 189

Nondeliberate Transparency 193

Comic Books and Eye Drops 195

The Ancient Olympic Oath 197

My Girl 203

A Rose a Day 207

Watch the Company You Keep 209

Come and Have a Better Seat 213

What Does God Prize? 215

Together We Are 130 Years Old 219

We Aren't Cheap, We're Thrifty 223

Night-Blooming Cereus 227

Where Is He? 229

The A-Team 233

A Lesser Life 237

Walking a New Path 239

Blessed to be a Blessing 243

Beach Walks and Shell Trees 247

I'd Love to Have a Pelican 249

Our Study 251

The Fosbury Flop 255

Grow Old with Me 257

Reminders 259

Daffodils Will Bloom Again 263

Remembering a Legacy 265

Oil Changes and Physical Therapy 269

Bring Forth the Royal Diadem 273

God's Nudges 277

ACKNOWLEDGMENTS

Thank you, Joyce Graham and Peggy Smith, for being proofreaders extraordinaire. Your gracious gifts of time and support are so appreciated.

Jan Woodard, you are an excellent tutor, and you helped me accomplish my goal. Thank you for being there and giving of your expertise and encouragement.

To my life group sisters and brothers, your prayers and love have meant so much to me. You held me close through a difficult time, and I am grateful.

A special thank you to my granddaughter, Michaela Bracken, 3 time PIAA State Medalist and Division 1 track and Field athlete at Bucknell University for allowing me to use her picture on the cover.

A thank you also to my daughter, Elizabeth Bracken, for being the photographer for this shot.

INTRODUCTION

On November 1, 2017, the love of my life, my soul mate, my best friend, and my ministry partner stepped over the threshold from this life into the next. He used to say that we each "live one life and we live it in two places." On that day, he moved from place number one to place number two, where he met his Lord and Savior, Jesus Christ, face-to-face. One of Bill's favorite Bible verses was 2 Timothy 4:7–8:

> I have fought the good fight, I have finished the race, I have kept the faith. Now there is in store for me the crown of righteousness, which the Lord, the Righteous Judge, will award to me on that day—and not only to me, but also to all who have longed for His appearing. (NIV)

My family and friends often reflect on how Bill ran his race. He was passionate, purposeful, persistent, and persevering. Bill was not perfect in his walk, but he knew he was a sinner saved by grace and was eternally grateful for God's redemption. He was a new creation after he met Jesus, and his life showed this transformation.

In the days that followed his home-going, I felt empty, alone, heartbroken, and numb, even knowing he was with the Lord and safe. Heaven and eternity with God are promised to those who know Jesus, so I never felt hopeless or despairing. I did feel like curling up into a ball in the corner of my sunporch and staying there.

"I'm finished, Lord. Take me home too."

As I agonized on those dark days, I felt God say to my heart, "Linda, Bill ran his race, and he ran it well. You also have a race to run. I have a plan for your life in this new season. You need to run your race."

These words were not earth-shattering, but they were unexpected. You see, Bill and I were a team. Yes, we each had individual ministries, but we seemed to do best and be most effective as a team. We enjoyed teaching and serving together, and we believed it was what God had called us to do. When you lose one member of the team, things dramatically change. It isn't a "team" anymore.

"Now what, Lord? I can't go on without my team leader, my coach, my partner, my husband, my love. He is the heart of my life and the heart of our ministry. Now what? How can I go on with half a heart?"

In the 1970s, Bill and I felt the Lord was telling us to have an "impact on people, one by one." We were passionate about sharing God's love with others and helping them grow in their relationship with Jesus. I soon realized in this new season of life that God's calling on my life had not changed; it had just been altered a bit. I was still supposed to have an "impact on people one by one." The Lord was still with me, and He would use me and provide all I needed, even without Bill physically here with me. God has been my strength, peace, and even joy as I am learning contentment in this season of life. He has provided the comfort and power for me to move forward even through tears.

For years I have wanted to write something. Bill and I together wrote *Our Family Journey* in 2013, where we combined pictures and text chronicling our family history. We gave that book to the family on our fiftieth wedding anniversary. It has been in my heart to write another book someday. That day seems to be here.

This book isn't primarily about the process of overcoming grief as a widow, although that is a big part of it. It isn't just a devotional book, although I pray that the reader will draw closer to God. It isn't an autobiography or a novel about me and my family. It is a book of memories, snapshots of things I have experienced and learned in life and ways I have seen the Almighty God work. It is a book of reflections.

The word *reflection* is defined by Google as "serious thought or consideration, contemplation, study, deliberation, pondering, meditation, musing, and rumination." Vocabulary.com says, "If you reflect on your past experiences, you look at them again, thoughtfully."

It is a book about Bill, the love of my life, and his love for me and for his Lord. My marriage to Bill was not perfect, but it was surely unique. I thank the Lord for giving him to me, and I want to honor him by sharing some of his heart. Other than his God, I knew Bill best.

It is a book about the Lord Jesus, my Redeemer and life-changer. He is alive and well, and He is working in the lives of ordinary men and women, drawing them into a relationship with Himself. I have seen this awesome God change my husband from a self-proclaimed heathen to a dedicated Christ-follower. I have experienced Him healing, delivering, and changing me, and I see this metamorphosis in countless others that I have known along my life journey. I want to write about God's hand in my life.

This is a love story. The love of a man and a woman for each other and the love of God as He works and changes His children.

I pray that I can bring encouragement and hope to my readers as they reflect along with me.

We each have a race to run. May we run it with purpose and joy.

CROSSING THE FINISH LINE

It was a sunny, crisp Saturday, October 28, 2017. We put on our down-filled jackets and hurried out the door on our way to Forest Hills High School near Johnstown to cheer for granddaughter Michaela as she ran cross-country in the District 6 meet. I confess I had never been to a cross-country meet before Michaela and her older brother, Caleb, had taken up the sport. It was exciting and unique. It took place outside rather than in a gym, and the participants ran a prescribed course across hill and dale to return 3.1 miles later and cross the finish line. Since this was Michaela's senior year, it was a crucial meet for her.

The fun part of watching the athletes was that we could stand wherever we chose. At the beginning, we positioned ourselves near the starting line so we could see the runners take off after the crack of the gun. Then we moved as quickly as we could to whatever point on the trail that we chose, ready to cheer the athletes as they ran by. Regardless of where we stood, we would not be able to see the entire course all at once. As a family, we usually spread out so we could yell our encouragements to Mick as she ran past us. After the gun began the race, we all dispersed to our chosen location, and Bill said, "I am going to the finish line. Some of the best races are seen from the finish line." No one thought anything about those words that day, but four days later, my husband did indeed go to the finish line.

On December 12, I was looking online with the hopes of discovering a clue as to what went wrong in Bill's body. I had ordered an autopsy because his death happened so quickly, and I knew I would always agonize over it if I did not know what happened. As I waited for the autopsy results, I wrote in my journal:

> How marvelous a creation is the human body that You, O Lord, have created. The stuff going on in Bill's body was complicated, and You allowed it all to work for twenty-one years, actually for forty-three years, since he discovered a problem at age thirty. Thank You, Lord, for all those years. I was together with him for them all. You were our strength and shield. You drew him to You before that point, when he was twenty-seven. That is a miracle right there! Hallelujah!

When I begin to have a pity party and focus on all the "life" that we didn't get to live together, I have begun to choose rather to thank God for all we did have. We got to raise our children to adulthood and see our grandchildren born and growing. We got to play with, teach, and nurture each of those grandkids as we enjoyed getting to know them as individuals. We got to live an incredibly adventurous life together and see God's plan for our marriage unfold. We experienced the joy of receiving God's grace and salvation and had time to serve Him together.

One day we each will reach that finish line. Life is short, whether we cross over that line at thirty, fifty-two, seventy-three, or ninety. God has given us the gift of life, and we don't get to choose when we cross that finish line. But we do get to choose how we run the race. I have a new appreciation now of how fleeting life is. I want to make every day count now, most of the time. I still give in to laziness and self-centered living more than I want to, but my mainspring has been altered. On a good day, and there are many good days, I remember that I will also cross that finish line when the Lord calls me home. Until then, I have a race to run.

FOR ALL THE SAINTS

Bill entered the Church Triumphant at 3:17 p.m., November 1, 2017. It just so happened to be All Saints Day. Some friends have said that for Bill to enter heaven on that particular day was especially appropriate. It brings a smile to my face when I think about it. But really, the word *saint* in Scripture is a term meaning all true believers, the whole number of the redeemed. All Saints Day is a time to remember those in our church fellowship that have died and gone to be with the Lord. Christians observe this day in different ways, but our faith teaches us that when we worship God, we do so in communion with all true believers, past, present, and future.

One of Bill's all-time favorite hymns was "For All the Saints," written by Anglican bishop William Walsham How in 1864. We sang it each All Saints Day over many years. I can still see Bill singing this wonderful song with raised hands, worshipping the God he loved. I chose to open his celebration of life service with that hymn.

For all the saints who from their labors rest,
Who Thee by faith before the world confessed,
Thy name, O Jesus, be forever blest.
Alleluia! Alleluia!

O blest communion, fellowship divine!
We feebly struggle, they in glory shine;
Yet all are one in Thee, for all are Thine.
Alleluia! Alleluia!

And when the strife is fierce, the warfare long,
Steals on the ear the distant triumph song,
And hearts are brave again, and arms are strong.
Alleluia! Alleluia!

From earth's wide bounds, from ocean's farthest coast,
Through gates of pearl streams in the countless host,
Singing to Father, Son, and Holy Ghost,
Alleluia! Alleluia!

Can't you just imagine the multitude of the redeemed streaming through the gates of heaven as they sing praises to our Triune God? Bill is among this host of believers, and you and I will be one day as our races come to an end. Alleluia!

FROM WAILING TO DANCING

Psalm 30:11–12 says, "You turned my wailing into dancing; you removed my sackcloth and clothed me with joy, that my heart may sing to you and not be silent. O LORD my God, I will give you thanks forever" (NIV).

I have never thought of myself as much of a wailer. A crier, yes. A tearful reflector, of course. But a wailer? Never... until now. Yes, I found myself so full of pain that I had to let it out. What a wail it was! I find that I am actually good at it. Good at a skill I never wanted to acquire.

Usually, I am fairly under control emotionally. I do feel intense emotions, but when I need to be in "administrative mode," I can pull it off very well. In the critical care unit, when I stood and watched my beloved take his last breath, I was "cool as a cucumber," as my mother used to say. I was calm and under control. It is hard to explain because I don't fully understand it myself. Did I not care? Why was I so unemotional? Am I truly this stoic?

I asked questions. I arranged for an autopsy. I called the funeral director to arrange for him to come and get Bill's earthly body. My son, Billy, offered to drive me home, but I declined his loving offer. I drove my own car home with son-in-law, Ed, in the front of the parade and daughter, Beth, behind me in their cars since they had come separately. I slept in my home by myself that first night and all others since then. Am I a superwoman? Absolutely not! Am I hard and coldhearted? I don't think so. I believe I was just covered with God's holy "numbness" that clothed and protected me from the unspeakable pain of loss in those early days. God knew I needed it. He held me close and gave me that great gift of peace in the midst of sorrow and upheaval. His peace that passes all understanding is something I truly have experienced.

Well-meaning people had told me to "stay busy" at the beginning of this grief journey. I knew that was only part of the remedy. I decided that I needed to be still, be quiet, be alone with Jesus and take whatever time needed for Him to heal my heart, mind, and body. Part of that healing process has been the "unexpected wail," or I guess it would be "wails." It is not like me, so hard to fathom, so emancipating and healing, this release of sound and sobs and tears.

My journal says, "As I left the party…alone…tears on the way home, I am finding that when I allow my emotions full rein, I cry and even wail. Your peace brings me back down and all is okay again. The hardest concept is the fact that this is life…for the rest of my life. Sometimes I get so full of grief with that thought. I want Bill here with me. It feels really weird moving into 2018 without him. It seems like I am leaving him behind. I don't like that."

The words of Psalm 30:11–12 contain a promise that God will turn those wails into songs of joy. I wail much less today than in those early days, but if I need to cry, I give myself permission. The Lord always fulfills His promises, and I do feel the healing and the joy and the removal of my sackcloth. One day I will be able to dance again and smile and laugh without my heart hurting. But in the meantime, I sit at His feet and drink in His love and healing.

EMPTY CLOSETS AND MEMORY QUILTS

What am I going to do with all of Bill's wrestling trophies? His clothes? His books and personal items? I think every widow asks herself similar questions. Since Bill went to heaven in the beginning of November, the holidays were right around the corner and brought with them a perfect time to "gift" some items. I picked what I wanted to keep myself, then I chose one of his trophies or medals for each of the kids and grandkids that I thought they would like. It was meaningful to me, and I enjoyed the process as much as one can enjoy anything early in the grief journey. It was important to me that our family members have something of his.

When we were all together for Thanksgiving that first year, I wanted the family to take any article of clothing that they wanted. It felt very weird not only to me but also to all of us. No one wanted to invade Bill's privacy and be combing through his closet and dresser drawers. They each found a few things, but you could cut the tension with a knife. I realized this was all too soon. We were all too raw. I shut the closet doors until a later time.

A special friend of mine, Karen, is a talented seamstress, and she mentioned to me that she would be pleased to make a memory quilt out of any of Bill's T-shirts that I chose. That was easy and less traumatic. I chose well and knew they would come back to me in a form that I could wrap around myself and cuddle. She also made several small pillows out of flannel shirts Bill had. They all were very special gifts and dear to my heart.

I began this difficult purging process again several months later by making a list of Bill's friends and special people in his life and choosing a tie or piece of wrestling memorabilia to give to them. I wrote a note, packaged them up, and mailed them out, slowly becoming aware of how healing this process was to my heart.

During this time frame, I began to assess which men at church were about Bill's size and shape. I approached them each and told them I was giving away Bill's clothes and I would be pleased if they would bring their wife and stop over to see if there was anything that worked for them. I also made it known I had clothes to give, and many people came to pick from the pile.

Then came the Salvation Army drop-off. It was perhaps the hardest of the "giveaways." Bill dressed professionally for most of his career and had nice sport coats, ties, and trousers. To just "throw them in the bin" did not cut the mustard. After having a major meltdown in my car as I sat in the parking lot behind the Salvation Army store, I collected myself well enough to call the store and explain that my husband's clothes were "nice things" that I couldn't just "drop in the bin." A lovely clerk came to the front of the store with a rolling cart where items could be hung up, and she carefully and respectfully took Bill's clothes and gave me a hug.

In this very act of giving away those precious items that my love had worn or used, I experienced God's comfort. What peace I felt as I hugged Howard, who was wearing Bill's shirt, and Dave, who was wearing his black topcoat, one Sunday morning. Kevin was helping direct parking in the church lot when he came up to me in Bill's sport coat. Gary and Bob wore Bill's ties and made sure I saw them. Mark had his work papers filed in Bill's briefcase. Pastor Ryan served communion in Bill's white clergy robe, and I felt the love of God as I received another hug.

THE MASHED POTATO DISASTER

Holidays are particularly difficult when the one you love best is absent. Thanksgiving came soon after Bill went to heaven, and we had a choice of whether to celebrate or not. Actually, it really was not a dilemma for me. Of course, we would get together and do our usual. Bill would not have wanted us to do less. Thanksgiving for our family is a turkey dinner with all the trimmings at our home with all the family attending. I love the whole event, cooking the turkey, setting the table, and hosting the family. I am not looking forward to the day that this task falls to a younger member.

In our early marriage, we traveled to Harrisburg and had Thanksgiving dinner at both my parents' home and Bill's parents' home. At first, we did both on the same day. That was brutal. At the noon meal, we paced ourselves so we would not eat too much and be stuffed for the rest of the day. Ever try doing that? We were hungry, and it all looked so good, but we dared not have seconds for fear of the big meal that loomed large a few hours in the future. So we tried not to overeat at noon, but we often did, and then we had to force-feed the equally delightful repast at six. It was no fun.

We then began to do Thanksgiving with my parents on Wednesday evening and Bill's parents on Thanksgiving Day. That was a much better plan. Since I never made my own turkey until my children had become adults and married, I had large shoes to fill when it became my turn to host. Both sets of our parents made great meals. I learned how to make a decent turkey dinner and have really enjoyed hosting all of us at our home. So to now give it up or say it is too sad without Bill was not my plan. Was it sad? Yes, it was. Did I shed tears while preparing and hosting? Yes, I did. Tears are cleansing and help release the pressure of grief so I let them flow when the occasion arises as it often does.

That first Thanksgiving without Bill started much like always. The turkey was stuffed and went in the oven about 6:00 a.m., and the other side dishes were made or reheated at the appropriate times. The table was set with our Thanks-giving-themed name tags made years ago by grandchildren Caleb and Michaela. Sometimes the turkey wings fell off the cardboard tags, but they were repaired as needed with a spot of glue. I love the tradition, even though we have empty seats today for Josh and Bill. Josh, our special-needs grandson, had gone to be with Jesus only six weeks before Bill. We all smile through our tears imagining Josh with a new mind and body.

This day I had the potatoes ready to be mashed when Ed and Beth arrived. Everyone was helping put water glasses and items from the refrigerator onto the table. Beth was on deck as the designated potato masher. I am used to cooking alone, so when too many people clog the kitchen, I get some-what rattled. By this time Billy, Deb, and Luke had arrived, and we tearfully asked Billy to do Bill's job of carving the turkey. As I drained the water from the potatoes, I placed them in the stainless steel bowl that goes with my KitchenAid mixer. I set the bowl on the appliance but got distracted before I had secured it for mashing. Beth moved in to do her job, assuming all was well.

The next thing I knew, we had semimashed potato bits hurling through the air all over the kitchen and all over us. After a second, realizing what had just happened, we all collapsed in laughter. Someone shouted, "When the chief is gone, all heck breaks loose!"

The mashed potato disaster brought much-needed comic relief to a sad day. We all imagined Bill in heaven watching and shaking his head in dismay with a smile on his face.

WHERE ARE THE MOUSETRAPS?

The garage was Bill's man cave, sort of. He didn't hang out there daily, but he did enjoy organizing his workbench, placing his tools on pegboards in orderly fashion and rejoicing that he had just the right gadget to use at the time it was needed. So often he would come in from doing a project and announce, "It is so great to have the right tools!"

Bill took good care of his belongings, and those in the garage were no exception. He kept them in tiptop shape. It reminded me of my territorial claim on my kitchen. I knew where things were, and I didn't expect anyone to rearrange without my permission. This was his garage, and he had dominion over it.

When Bill went to heaven, the garage became my responsibility. It was another of those things I wished were not under my authority, but it was. In those first few months, I would just look at the garage from wall to wall as I was coming and going, taking notice of the order in it all. Everything had a place, and everything was in its place. It was Bill's. He was superorganized, and I could see his personality everywhere. His baseball caps were on the coatrack, and his jackets hung along the wall. A spray can of Bill's favorite antiseptic was on the shelf where he left it. This can was a cure-all for cuts and scrapes, and our kids grew up loving it. Not! It worked well to prevent infection but had a powerful sting when applied. I had no right to mess with his garage or change it in any way. But now it was mine, and I needed to know what was there and where things were that I might need.

I had begun feeding birds that first winter. I enjoyed seeing the various types I would attract at the bird feeder outside my sunroom window. I knew that it was important for me to store the seed in a container that could not be accessed by any varmint that might find its way into my garage uninvited. Knowing and doing are two different things. One bag of thistle was left unsecured for a day or two until I was able to get a bin for storage. One morning, I discovered little chew marks on the thistle bag. Immediately I wanted to ask Bill, "Where are the mousetraps?" But of course I couldn't.

I searched the whole garage and couldn't find any mousetraps anywhere. Writing it down on my trusty shopping list, I went on with the plans of my day. The next morning, I decided to run to the grocery store to get the needed traps and opened the house door to enter the garage and get into my car. There on the path to my car, near the thistle bag, was a dead mouse.

"Lord, I thank You so much. You took care of the mouse, and I didn't even have to set or empty a trap. I am grateful," I said to God very appreciatively.

Because I needed to dispose of the trespasser, my mind began racing as to the best way to do that. I decided I couldn't bring myself to pick it up with a gloved hand, so I needed to put some space between me and the body. Aww! One of Bill's tools could help. I selected a needle-nosed plier that he had taught me about and carefully guided it toward the mouse's tail with plans to clamp and dispose. I almost lost my breakfast when the mouse wiggled as I clamped onto his tail. The mouse was only half-dead! My heart was in my throat, and again I asked Bill where he was when I needed him!

I could not bear to watch the mouse expire, so I did not use the car that day. The next morning, I repeated steps 1, 2, and 3 again, but this time no wiggle. The deed was done, and I did buy more traps just in case this guy had other family members. The garage was now mine to steward.

THIS IS THE DAY

This is the day that the Lord has made; let us rejoice and be glad in it.

—Psalm 118:24 NIV

We sang a chorus based on this verse years ago at our Bethel Covenant Community Prayer and Praise meetings held in our great room upstairs in Brush Valley. I can still see our children and our Bethel family as they clapped and belted out the words to this song. It was a rousing tune that called us all to remember that God had given us the good gift of life in that day and it was our job to be grateful as we lived in it. Over the years, Christian songwriters updated the melody and lyrics several times, but the message was still the same.

Recently, this verse has taken on new meaning for me and my family. Bill had this verse as the greeting on his cell phone. I wish I could hear it again in his voice, but we canceled the service on the phone after he went to heaven. Don't think he has need of it there! I bought a metal sign of this verse, and it hangs on my bedroom wall. Seeing a wooden plank containing this verse, I had to have it for our South Carolina home. On the first of the month, I often text, "This is the day…" to my daughter and son, in memory of Bill, since he went to heaven on November 1.

I wonder why he chose it to put on his phone. Could it be that we need to remind ourselves that God has given us life and breath? Maybe it was to celebrate the fact that we had lived another day and God was with us. No day should be taken for granted, because we aren't promised a certain number of them. We humans tend to need a reminder that regardless of what each day holds, the Lord is there and we have the privilege of rejoicing in the good times and in the bad. I don't know why he chose it, but I do know why it is important to me now.

It reminds me of Bill whenever I hear or read it. It also reminds me that God holds my life tightly in the hollow of His hand. Nothing can separate me from the love of God in Christ Jesus our Lord, Scripture reminds me in Romans 8. It challenges me that my only reasonable response to this gift is to rejoice and be glad. Rejoice on days that are mundane and ordinary. Rejoice on days that are full of laughter and fun. And especially rejoice on days like November 1, 2017, when everything changes, heartbreak comes, and the future looks dim.

ADVENTURE WAS HIS
MIDDLE NAME

Sometimes a teacher will have the attendees of a class inter-act with the presented material in some way. "Make a list of…" "Write down all the ways that…" "Tell about a time when you…" These are good techniques to elicit ownership and response from those listening.

One of the hardest and yet most meaningful things that I am having to do in this new season of life called widow-hood is to go through things of Bill's that I never had seen before. We did not have secret stashes from each other, but he respected my journal entries as my private talks with the Lord, and I gave him that same respect. Now, all is fair game. It feels a bit weird and invasive.

One class we attended together encouraged us to finish this sentence-starter, "I am a person who…" The answers to these and similar open-ended statements help us understand ourselves better and also help others to know us more fully. Bill had answered with things like, "I am a person who tries to serve the Lord," "I am a person who loves my wife," and "I am a person who loves to play with my grandchildren." All these sentence endings speak of who Bill was, but one particular sentence he wrote was so telling of his personality. "I am a person who loves adventure."

Anyone who had spent even a short amount of time with Bill came to know that he loved anything that hinted of adventure. His full name was William A. Blacksmith III, with the *A* standing for his middle name, August. I often thought it should have stood for Adventure because he epitomized that word. He wasn't fond of hiking trails that came to an end and required you to hike back the same path. No, he wanted to discover new paths. Over the years, he developed and taught new adventure courses at Indiana University of Pennsylvania in the area of backpacking, rock climbing, and downhill skiing. He wrote a list for the grandchildren that he titled "Seventy-Two Things to Do at Grami and Papa's House" so he could keep the action moving. Bill wanted to teach the grandkids how to kayak, so we had to buy several kayaks. Notice I didn't tell you exactly how many he bought! Think big!

He excelled in just about every physical pursuit he attempted, but adventure for him was not limited to sports. He went to seminary in his forties and retired from a career he loved to begin anew in full-time ministry when he was sixty. He retired for a second time to continue to seek what the Lord had for him when he was seventy. Bill experienced the beginning of kidney failure when he was thirty, went on dialysis at the same time he was playing recreational ice hockey, and had a kidney transplant when he was fifty-two.

A friend said to me after Bill went to heaven, "Linda, you should write a book about all the adventures you and Bill had in your marriage." I pondered and prayed about that statement often. God surely gave Bill a life that matched his heart and personality. I have to smile when I think of all the adventure that he is now experiencing in the presence of his Lord and Savior

SAVE THE PIE!

The year was 1955, and I was so excited as several of my friends and I piled into the back seat of Sharon's dad's Buick. We called him Judge, although he was not a real judge. Sharon was my best friend and neighbor. Our destination was a large hunting cabin that Judge and some others owned, and we were blessed to be able to occupy it for a few days. Lots of giggling ensued as the ten-year-old girls planned their itinerary. The moms decked us all out with the hot dogs and buns and every other goody that little girls might enjoy. My mom sent a pumpkin pie.

Driving down the lane to the camp, we moved under a canopy of brightly colored leaves as the trees lined the right and the left of the narrow road. As we approached the cabin, I was amazed by its size. It was more like a hunting mansion than a cabin. A two-story structure, part stone and part wood, stood in the clearing. We drove into the driveway slowly, and when the car stopped, we quickly piled out and were on a dead run for the door when Judge yelled for us to halt.

"I'm going to build a fire in the fireplace to warm us up while you girls head upstairs and pick your bunk for the weekend," he announced as he jumped out of the car. "Before you go, pick up your suitcase and take it with you. I'll bring in the food boxes."

The weather was crisp and sunny, and we rushed up the steps to the second floor and "Oohed" and "Ahhed" our way around the bedrooms. I chose my bunk right next to Sharon's and began to unload my suitcase. I was excited to get ready to wear the flannel shirt my dad loaned me. It would be big, but I felt so grown-up in it.

Not much time passed when Judge bolted up the stairs screaming that we needed to hurry and get out.

"The cabin is on fire!" he cried. "Leave everything here. Just get yourself out."

Although I knew I needed to listen to him, I reached down and picked my Bible out of my suitcase. It was a gift from my grandma Lettie, and I didn't want it to perish. Wish I had grabbed my dad's flannel shirt as well!

As we ran to the kitchen door, I reached out to save the pie! (My family will find this funny, but that is another story.) Actions are not rational at times like this. Three little girls never ran so fast in their lives! Nor did this middle-aged man! In what seemed like seconds, the cabin was full of smoke, and flames darted out the windows. Judge felt he could not fight the blaze because his first responsibility was to keep his young passengers protected. He started the car and drove a safe distance away from the cabin to watch but be out of danger.

And watch we did! By the time we left, the foundation and stone side walls were all that was standing. On our quiet journey home, I opened my Bible and looked at the passage before me in Psalm 4:8, which said,

"I will lie down and sleep in peace, for you alone, O LORD, make me dwell in safety" (NIV).

I think this was the first time I realized that God speaks and cares so intimately for His children. Thank You, Lord.

NO WAVES ALLOWED

The beach at Murrells Inlet, South Carolina, is beautiful with its tan sand and mild waves. We noticed right away that, unless there was a storm brewing, the surf in this part of South Carolina is much calmer than the tumbling, wipeout waves we were used to seeing in New Jersey. Waves are an expected part of the beach scene, but waves in my life were not welcomed.

I define a *wave* as anything that causes my stomach to turn over, my heart to palpitate, and my internal world to tumble like a dryer full of clothes. Waves came to me as a child in various forms, but one wave I vividly remember is when my homelife was disturbed. Mom and Dad were loving, kind, and generous to my brother and me. They also loved each other, but like all married couples, they occasionally had arguments. What's the big deal? It shouldn't have been an issue, but when I was in first or second grade, I couldn't emotionally handle disagreements and arguments. I became so distressed that I came up with an ingenious idea to stop all verbal assaults. I would go into the closet, close the door, and begin to scream. Now you'll have to agree that it probably was effective!

When this happened, my parents would hurry to find me, coax me out of the closet, and the arguments would stop. Pretty good manipulation, I'd say! Please don't think my parents were always bickering and shouting at each other, because they weren't. They were both caring and gentle, but I just could not handle "waves." I wish they had been able to take me in their arms and hug me and share that disagreements were a part of life, but I don't think they had the emotional wherewithal to do that. They grew up in an era where emotions were kept inside, and I don't think they knew how to help me.

I eventually grew out of the screaming phase but still tried to avoid conflict of any kind. If my friends hurt my feelings, I would cry and pack up my dolls and go home. One junior high friend insulted me, and I choked down my sobs as I ran from her. I had not learned how to stand up to insults or how to confront when something was wrong or even how to understand myself and what I was feeling. I was a classic "people pleaser," and I was very good at it. I reasoned that if I did what people wanted, then they would like me and there would be no angry words to deal with. I had life all figured out, or so I thought.

I was voted Most Popular Girl by my high school classmates my senior year. That was a nice honor to have, but as I look at it now, it is so telling of where I was emotionally at that time. Well, of course everyone liked me! I never challenged them or disagreed with them or took a stand on anything they said or did. Bill used to say that in our early marriage, he had it made! I agreed with him on most everything, and so life was hunky-dory. Or was it?

As I grew as a Christian, and as Bill and I grew as a couple, I learned that waves were as natural in life as they are in the ocean. We are all sinful humans who do not always do things correctly, so conflict is part of life. God began to bring healing to that scared, confused little girl. I learned to handle conflict without withdrawing or crying—well, most of the time. I discovered that I had some preferences, a few opinions, and several ideas that I even felt passionate about. Disagreement became tolerable for me, although not sought-after. Bill and I began to learn how to handle our conflicts, and our marriage was ever so much better because of it. He teasingly reminded me of how great it was when I agreed with everything he did or said!

"That's not going to happen anymore," I would quickly remind him.

FOR AN AUDIENCE OF ONE

Bill used to remind our granddaughter Michaela, who ran in cross-country and track, that she was running for "an audience of one." As God watched her run, she needed only to please Him. What good advice that is for all of life, not only athletics! So many of us live life seeking to please others more than pleasing God.

As a child, I was very shy. My mother said that when I was introduced to new people, I would just stare at them with a frown on my face. I was self-conscious. And fearful too. I told my parents that the boys in kindergarten gave me a headache, so I would turn around and walk home before I even got to school. Those were the days when kids were allowed to walk the several blocks to school without parents being with them. Mom would head me back out the door and remind me that it was my job to be in school. I did make the trek to school, but with a nervous heart.

I remember feeling afraid and anxious about speaking in front of my class in junior high and high school. What would they think of me? Would I measure up to their standards? Would I perform as well as they did? My fears were many, and one was that I might not be able to talk. That seems such a weird fear to me now, but it was very real when I was thirteen. To prepare myself for class, I would rehearse hearing my voice over and over before I got to school. Oh my! I wish now I could go back and share some wisdom with that young girl.

I read a book recently called *The Lies Women Believe*, by Nancy DeMoss Wolgemuth, and she identifies forty lies that Satan would have women (but I think anyone) believe that either skew or pervert God's truth. For me, one of the lies I have fought against my whole life is that I need to please everyone. No one can please everyone. It is a lie that if I do what people expect of me, they will, in turn, like me. It is also a lie that if I don't make waves in the sea of life, I will be happy. That is not true.

These are lies from the pit of hell and can cause us great harm if we believe them and let them infect our hearts. Our lives are created by God, and He is our Redeemer and Sustainer. If I know that God created me and understands my emotionality, then it follows that He is aware of my struggles and my pain. What others believe about me or expect of me is not nearly so important as what He wants me to do or be. Although He has put us in communities and in relationships, our allegiance and our loyalty are primarily to Him and not to others. We can never make everyone happy, even though we may try. Our job is to treat others like Jesus would treat them and let the chips fall where they may.

I was well into adulthood when I came face-to-face with this lie. I don't think I was even aware of my disfunction in my youth, but God was. He began to allow me to see that I did not need to please those around me. Growth so often comes as a result of pain.

POM POMS AND MEGAPHONES

I grew up very shy and fearful, but I loved cheerleading. Somehow that seems strange to me to be so timid but enjoy the "up-frontness" of leading a cheering crowd. Oh well! I was so sure I would be a cheerleader in sixth grade, but we moved and I could not try out for the squad. I was equally sure I would be a cheerleader in ninth grade, but we moved, so I could not try out, again. The new high school, Cedar Cliff, was a jointure of West Shore and New Cumberland, and those in ninth grade from both schools could try out to be a cheerleader for tenth grade in the new high school. The problem was, they were only picking two sophomores. Among all those girls, and so many that had been junior high cheerleaders, I didn't have a chance. I know this is shallow and very unimportant in the whole scheme of things in this world, but I believe that the Lord granted me the desire of my heart. I tried out and secured one of the sophomore spots. It was indeed a happy day at my house!

In my school, if you served as a cheerleader in tenth grade, you automatically stayed on the squad for the remainder of high school. Sweet! I felt it was a dream come true, and I thoroughly enjoyed this extracurricular activity. My parents would say I majored in cheerleading and attended my academic classes on the side. (I was actually an A/B student and did well in most of my classes except algebra. I had to take that subject for a second time in summer school so I would be ready to advance to algebra II the next year.)Cheerleading actually has something to do with how Bill and I got together. Since he was a wrestler, he didn't frequent basketball games too often because they were both winter sports. I cheered at the basketball games. In January of 1962, Bill attended a game with his best friend, Bob. In typical male conversation about girls, Bob mentioned that I had recently broken up with my longtime boyfriend and Bill should consider asking me out on a date. Ever so observant, Bill responded that he had never noticed me before. I was one of the shortest cheerleaders, so I was way down on the right end of the cheering line. On that evening, he did take notice and planned his approach to securing a date with me.

I got wind of the upcoming "ask," so I was prepared when his call came. That was way before cell phones, and I had an extension phone in my bedroom, long cord and all.

"Hi, Linda. This is Bill."

I wanted to be cool, so I responded, "Bill who?" I know, it was a cheesy retort! I did not want him to know I was thrilled that this very cute star wrestler invited me out. I tried to be calm, but my heart was racing.

Our first date was just a ride home from a school event. He walked me to my door and kissed my forehead before departing. Oh, my! There was never a more romantic gesture on record than that. I was hooked.

We dated for a couple of months, and Bill asked me to "go steady" with him on March 4. That date was important, and we celebrated it each year right along with our wedding date of June 28. I still do something special to celebrate both days. Last year I bought myself perfume on our actual anniversary. Before you judge how self-centered that was, I remind you that Bill would have done just that. So I did!

A PROPHETIC UTTERANCE

God speaks to our hearts in various places and in unusual ways. One of the funny stories when we were dating was Bill's first sense that I might be the "one and only" for him. He recalled one evening, walking past the washer and dryer—or was it the refrigerator?—sensing that God was speaking to him. This is unique because Bill, at that point, was not a serious God-follower. I don't think he ever experienced anything like this before.

I'm going to marry that girl, he thought. He had never contemplated that scenario and was surprised by the idea. Even though we had been dating a while, marriage was not yet part of his mental wheelhouse.

Of course, I loved this when he shared it with me. He knew ahead of time that I was the one, that I was his true love! How romantic! How prophetic! All of it was good except the possible visual of me spending untold future hours treating stained T-shirts and folding mounds of towels. After all, this revelation came by the washer and dryer! Was there any connection?

Even worse was the thought of me having a love affair with the refrigerator. If my family is reading this book, and I hope they do, they should get a kick out of that second image. Although I am slim as a willow (*not*), there is a running joke among my not-so-sensitive relatives that I love to eat. Especially *pie*! That is another story that is really not worthy of sharing, so I won't. I do love to eat, though. When we fell in love, I weighed 105 pounds. That is a nostalgic memory of days gone by…way by! No one told me that you can't gain a pound a year and still stay tiny. In my senior years, I am trying to reverse that trend.

My certainty of Bill being my future husband was not nearly as dramatic as his. There were no appliances involved! During my senior year, I remember scrawling his name on my notebooks and even adding "Mrs. William A. Blacksmith." I think most teenage girls do that type of thing when they are in love. I had no words coming from the heavens to confirm my heart's desire, but I loved it that he did. I also loved that God had all this figured out way ahead of us.

Psalm 139:13–14 says, "For you created my inmost being; You knit me together in my mother's womb. I praise You because I am fearfully and wonderfully made" (NIV).

His perfect plan is perfect. I'd love to tell you that we were perfect actors in God's drama, but we weren't. We were married at the end of my senior year, when I was eighteen and Bill was nineteen. Our firstborn child came into the world five months later.

WRESTLING WITH LOVE

We spent as much time together that year as we could. We went to wrestling matches of other teams (not surprising); we went to movies, parties, and dances. September came, and Bill was off to college at Lock Haven. As his parents' car pulled away from his freshman dorm room on move-in day, I saw Bill cry for the first time. We were both heartbroken to be separated. To solve the problem, he would hitchhike from Lock Haven to Harrisburg on weekends whenever he wasn't involved with wrestling. I was a high school senior that year, and on occasion I would be allowed to go to his college to visit. Fortunately, I had a friend who lived in Lock Haven, so I could visit her and also see Bill.

It was fun traveling to see Bill's wrestling matches. My dad got into the spirit of it all and drove me to his matches on occasion. Bill's brother Jim and his now wife, Jody, were my traveling buddies most often. It is great when family members are also friends.

Bill and I went to church with my parents when he came home on weekends. We talked about God once in a while and knew each other were believers, even though Bill did not really understand who this Jesus fellow was. He had come from a family that did not regularly attend church. Even though I was a bit ahead of him in the spirituality department, neither of us knew how much God loved us. We did not know how to please Him or live according to His Word.

We were very much in love, and I found myself pregnant. In today's world, this is not as shocking a situation as it was in 1963. I was in my senior year, at a time when colleges were being considered and plans were being made by my classmates. I applied to schools like my friends did, knowing I probably would not be attending. I think I was in denial for so long, and Bill and I decided to just keep quiet about things for as long as we could. Since I was tiny then, my growing tummy did not really show. I went through finals, end-of-school parties, and graduation without missing a beat.

We needed to face reality, so the time finally came to tell our parents. I was so ashamed that I had to hurt my parents so much. They were proud, professional people, and this kind of thing was not accepted well in those days. In reality, this was not God's plan for us either. Even though we were not walking with Jesus at this time, both Bill and I knew this was not His best for either of us, not then and not ever.

Both sets of parents were loving and accepting of us as we moved forward. Since we both declared our love for each other and our desire to be together, we were married in a small ceremony on June 28, 1963. Bill was nineteen, and I was eighteen, just kids ourselves. Our sweet son was born just five months later. Since we were so young, people often thought we were the babysitters for our son, Billy. I know our parents were holding their collective breath during those early years. After Bill became a Christian, he wrote my parents a letter, asking their forgiveness.

This kind of a start to a marriage is not ideal, but God has a way of taking our mistakes, our sin, and providing forgiveness and redemption. Because He is faithful, we grew as a couple and as a family. Because He is in the transforming business, we were changed as His Holy Spirit worked in our hearts. He took two immature teenagers and made them new creations in Him. We would not have made it on our own. I am eternally grateful for His mercy and grace.

POOL BALLS A-FLYING

In our early married years, we did not have a lifestyle like most college students. We were young, but we had a son, Billy. Most of our potential friends were footloose and fancy-free, and most of the parents of infants were much older. We were kind of in no-man's-land as far as friends went. We wanted more companions, but they were hard to find. Bill's brother Jim and Jody became our best buddies. Jim was enrolled at Lock Haven, and Jody transferred there, so we really spent a lot of time together.

Our foursome plus Billy played, laughed, and just hung out together. Jim and Jody loved their nephew, and he loved them. We played cards, took walks, and ate ice cream cake roll from Jimmy's Store (no connection to Jim) up the street. We often would purchase two cake rolls. The three of us would split one of them, and one was for Bill alone. That guy could put away the ice cream!

One funny memory stands out to me when I think of those early married years. Bill and I came "home" to Harrisburg on weekends when we could. A lot of our high school friends were still around, and we enjoyed connecting with them. We would hang out at Bill's parents' home, where a pool table graced their basement.

Jim and Jody were often there when we were, and the men frequently enjoyed a competitive game of pool. This one evening, Jody and I were dutifully watching the prowess of our guys as they aimed and took their shots. I was very pregnant. I felt like I had a beach ball in my lap when I sat down. At that stage, I was quite uncomfortable but wanted to be part of the evening activities anyway. After a few calm games, the contest escalated quickly to something more challenging, which was no surprise when these two brothers were together. Remember, they were both wrestlers and never wanted to lose.

Instead of using the pool cue to propel the pool balls, as was the typical way, they decided it would be fun to roll the balls using their hands and try to hit those of their opponent, which would in turn send balls propelling every which way. They quickly found that the harder they pushed the ball, the bigger the smash. The taunting and gloating got louder and louder as the pool balls spun out of control. All of a sudden, Jody and I found ourselves in a war zone. The projectiles stayed on the table, fortunately, but they were moving with such fury that I covered my beach ball tummy with my arms and hoped to stay alive. You may be asking yourself why the ladies didn't just get out of Dodge. I think we might have been afraid to move, or maybe it was because we were laughing so hard.

Oh, to be young and carefree again!

IT WAS SUPPOSED TO BOUNCE!

The year was 1966, and we had been living on Water Street in Indiana for about four months. The moving boxes had been unpacked, and things settled in. Neither Bill nor I liked clutter, so we found places for everything in short order. Other years, as students, we spent the holidays at our parents' homes and helped them decorate their trees. We never had one of our own.

In our new rental home, we were delighted to be able to have our very own tree but realized it would be bare—we didn't own any decorations. Ever generous, both sets of parents downsized their stash of string lights and ornaments, and we returned home to Indiana one weekend with all we needed to decorate up a storm. It actually was really fun because we each could identify favorite things from our childhood that we now brought into our together life.

We decided to begin a new tradition of selecting and cutting down our own tree, which made perfect sense in Indiana, Pennsylvania, which was called the Christmas Tree

Capital of the World. Billy was old enough to enjoy the process, and we spent way too many hours making our selection that blustery Saturday.

"This one is too tall!"

"That one is skinny as a rail!"

"This one looks like a Charlie Brown tree. Look how it leans."

We finally found the perfect blue spruce, which we tied to the top of our car as we sang Christmas carols all the way home. Once the evergreen was firmly situated in its stand, we started to sort through the boxes of donated Christmas paraphernalia. Bill spied the angel that had graced the top of his family tree. I found several strings of colored lights that I recognized as my dad's favorite kind. One by one we lifted each treasure carefully from the boxes to share with each other our memories.

I was so excited to discover a couple of older ornaments that my family had used for as long as I remembered. One particular ball was purple glass and had a yellow stripe around its middle. I was so thrilled to now have it for our first tree together as a married couple, and I carefully scoped out a place to hang it.

"Look at this, Bill. See how it reflects the light! I remember this ball on my tree at home. Isn't it beautiful?"

Bill turned to me at that point and took the ball from my hand and said, "Hey, we had one just like this. Watch what it can do!"

Before I could react or gasp or grab it back, he had taken the ball from me and threw it on the hardwood floor in a movement reminiscent to the throwing of a yo-yo. Shards of glass exploded everywhere, and we both stood there stunned. I actually had no words. What had just happened? Why would Bill do such a thoughtless thing to this special ornament? *I can't believe this!*

"The one I had bounced," he sheepishly uttered. "I am so very sorry."

While I now understood the reason for the disaster before me on the floor, I was dumbfounded. Later in the tree-decorating scenario, we found in his family box the identical ball to mine that he had remembered.

It did, indeed, bounce!

MACARONI SALAD

Money was scarce in those early days of married life, so vacations were taken in our tent. Later, we purchased a used camper that we fondly named Agarn. One time we invited my parents, Bam and Pop, to go along on a camping trip. My dad enjoyed sharing how he kept slipping down to the bottom of the cot, wearing his silk pj's, because we pitched the tent on a slight incline. My question was, "Who wears silk pajamas on a camping trip?"

Another time, we went with Bill's parents, Hon and Pop, along with my brother Ned, who came to be a helper to us by watching his cute nephew. Ned recalls it as being a "sweet deal" for him. Playing on a sailboat with Bill during the day and watching Billy if we went out in the evening. Free vacation!

One particularly eventful vacation was with Jim and Jody at Stone Harbor. We were able to afford splitting the cost of a small rental outside of the resort town and were packed and ready for a great week in the sun. We couldn't wait to hit the beach, swim, and build the obligatory sandcastle. I fully expected the competition between the brothers would rear its head as they would battle the ocean to defend their elaborate sandcastle against the incoming tide.

After the first day of lovely weather and typical beach activities, we faced the remaining six days, which called for heavy rain. The backyard became a pool of water, and we soon tired of cards and board games. Those once-good spirits disappeared as we found ourselves becoming bored, and monotony soon set in.

Each day felt the same as we waited for the sun to come out once again. Toward the end of the week, we were eating lunch while watching the downpour outside. Love and generosity were wearing thin for all of us. In the meal conversation, one of the brothers challenged the other with some sort of verbal provocation.

"If you say that again, I'm going to throw the macaroni salad at you!"

Now, this was not a small bowl of macaroni salad. It was ample and creamy and delicious. As soon as I heard the dare, I knew we were in trouble. I knew these two could not resist the encounter. Without missing a beat, the other brother promptly took the dare, said it again, and very soon the bowl of macaroni salad was lifted from the table and the contents heaved across the kitchen as promised. Rex, our dog, sure enjoyed the event. I don't remember if we laughed or cried as we *all* cleaned up the mess, but it sure brings a smile to my face now. Yes, it was wasteful, juvenile, impulsive, dumb even. But it was two very competitive brothers doing what boys sometimes do.

You noticed I have not told you which brother threw the food! Maybe you can guess.

DRIVE UP ALONG THE SIDEWALK

Remember, if it smacks of adventure, Bill was "in," and since he was my best friend, I was often "in" also. We belonged to a group of families from church that owned a camp not far from Indiana. The dads, a few moms, most of the teens and older kids all owned and ran their dirt bikes up and down the bony piles around the camp. For readers who are not from Western Pennsylvania, a *bony pile* is a mound of coal waste the size of a large hill. Those hills made great recreation for riders who have the intestinal fortitude to get a head start and race up the hill on their bikes, hoping to reach the top, swerve around, and head back down.

Bill and seven-year-old Billy had bikes and wanted me to join them in the sport. This was prior to Beth coming into the world. Carefully, Bill chose a used dirt bike with minimum horse power for me so I would be safe. He patiently taught me all the ins and outs of riding, and I practiced each weekend with the family, either at the camp or in the countryside surrounding our home. I got pretty confident in my ability, and I felt I was ready to get my license to ride on the road.

Now, before you get the wrong idea, I never intended to be a motorcyclist on the highway. We both just felt it best to have that certification in case we chose to go from place A to place B and needed to be on a country road. How hard can it be to get the motorcycle stamp on your driver's license? After all, I was a semi-intelligent adult and had been driving a car for a number of years.

The motorcycle test day started fine. We took my dirt bike on our trailer as we drove to the test site in Homer City. A nice young officer came out to the curb to talk with me and tell me what he wanted me to do. I found myself more nervous than I had anticipated, mostly because both Bill and Billy were watching.

My first task was to do figure eights in the parking lot. No problem! As all eyes were on me, I began to push down on the pedal to kick-start the bike. I had done it hundreds of times, so no big deal. This time it wouldn't start. I jumped on that starter again and again, but nothing. The sweet officer leaned over to me and said, "Ma'am, it might work better if you turned on the key."

So now I was mortified. I turned on the key, jumped down on the pedal, and my bike started up right away. Whew! I easily did my figure eight maneuver with no worries. *I can do this!* I thought.

The next thing he asked me to do was to drive along the sidewalk to the end of the road then come back. The sidewalk was narrow, so I was nervous doing this one, but I did it. I didn't know until I came back and saw the horrified look on everyone's faces that the policeman had wanted me to actually drive *on* the road that bordered *along* the sidewalk, not drive *on* the sidewalk.

Bill so enjoyed sharing this story and embellished it by saying that I nearly killed a little old lady who was walking on the sidewalk at that time. You guessed it. That last part didn't happen.

I passed my motorcycle test. Bill said it was because I was cute.

CAMP SOLES

For God so loved the world that He gave His one and only Son, that whoever believes in Him shall not perish but have eternal life.

—John 3:16 NIV

I was teaching first grade at Benjamin Franklin Elementary School in Indiana, Pennsylvania, in 1971, when Barb, the mom of one of the little girls in my class, began to share with me about Graystone Church's Labor Day retreat. She invited Bill and me to consider attending. At that point in history, we had joined Graystone and were regularly attending but were not very involved. Bill had come from a family of church members but nonattenders. He had no interest in retreats of any kind, so I was reluctant to even ask him about it. Barb seemed to know how to woo us, because she told me about all the sport activities at Camp Soles, such as volleyball, canoeing, basketball, softball, etc. Of course, I passed this information on to Bill, hoping he would be as drawn to the idea of going as I was.

After a bit of negotiating, we did sign up with the provision that we would bring our camper as our sleeping accommodations. Billy was almost eight years old, and I was pregnant with Beth. We packed up on Friday and headed for the Laurel Highlands of Western Pennsylvania, expecting a long weekend of fun and games. God had other plans for us.

The retreat was structured such that we had morning and evening teaching sessions, but most of the afternoon was free for participating in sports events, and participate Bill did! He was an athlete and good at almost anything he tried. This was a place very close to heaven for my sports-loving husband. The teaching sessions were on the topic of God's love, and they were taught by a visiting pastor. I was encouraged by the teacher, and Bill seemed to be listening. I had no idea until later the depth of his interest or the softening of his heart.

By the time Sunday evening rolled around, another teacher and topic were introduced. Jack, a Graystone elder who later became Bill's close friend and mentor, was sharing on the topic of the Holy Spirit. At the end of his presentation, he wisely invited anyone that wanted to give their life to Jesus to stand up. Guess what? My sweet husband stood up! I was shocked and very nervous. Bill later said that I probably thought he was going to walk out. For years I had been praying for my husband to come to know Jesus, but when this happened, I found myself surprised. Why do we do that? We pray and then are amazed when He answers!

This was Bill's time to meet the Master. I think he was the only one on his feet, and Jack asked some of us sitting near to Bill to stand and lay hands on him. There were six or eight people surrounding Bill as Jack led him through the "sinner's prayer." Bill confessed his need for the Lord's forgiveness and invited Jesus to come into his heart. All hands were on Bill's shoulders. Later, my husband told me that during the prayer, he felt a strong hand laid on his head. He popped up his eyes to look but saw everyone still in their original places and their hands still on his shoulders. We believe that God had miraculously touched Bill during that prayer, touched his head because he needed that assurance and touched his heart to be forever changed.

LORD, HEAR MY PRAYER

At that same Labor Day retreat, I recommitted my life to the Lord. Up until that time, I had been playing spiritual games. Although I was raised in a Christian home and we were at church every Sunday morning, Jesus was not yet real to me. Spirituality in my home consisted of grace before each meal and bedtime prayers. As I look back on that period, something seems strange to me. My mom and dad read their Bibles each day. I saw them doing it, but I don't remember them teaching me about this discipline or talking at all about having a personal relationship with God. Maybe that reflects how sterile family life was in those days, or maybe just my family life. We were a loving family, but not a nurturing one. We did not talk with one another about our feelings or emotions. "Keep your own counsel," some have called it.

Although we attended a Presbyterian church and my dad was an elder and my mom was a Sunday school teacher, I never gave my heart to Jesus. A school friend's dad was a pastor, and he decided to start a club for kids after school called the Golden Cross Club. I attended because it was right up the street from my house. I know I had heard the gospel before, but I really "heard" it there for the first time. This time I understood about Jesus loving me and dying on the cross to save me from my sin. He paid the price for me. His resurrection made it possible for me to live eternally in heaven with Him if I became one of His children. My ears were open, and so was my heart, as I prayed a prayer of surrender to Jesus at age nine.

During my teen years, I often read my Bible before I went to bed, and I tried to live like He wanted, but I failed. That Labor Day brought me to a place of being honest with myself and God. I had said the words but had not surrendered all as a child. I was ready to be serious now as a twenty-six-year-old expectant mother in September 1971.

Life's journey continued as I began to learn about spending time with the Lord each day. Some call it a quiet time or upper room time or morning watch. It is simply a time of Bible reading, study, meditation, and prayer. It is being alone with God to get to know Him better.

One of the disciplines I began to do in the eighties was journaling. I would write the activities of the day, my prayers, my concerns, and my dreams. I would jot down anything I felt the Lord sharing with my heart. I have kept those journals from 1980 onward. I didn't write every single day but often enough to see a pattern developing as God was pruning me, encouraging me, holding me close, and being patient with me as I grew and as I failed.

Looking back over the journals is both edifying and humbling. I rejoice when I see growth in my character and lifestyle and am brought to my knees when I see besetting sin appear again and again with no visible change in my character. My life verse comes from Philippians 1:6, where God promises to complete the work in me that He started. Even if I fail again and again, He is at work in me and He will complete it until the day Jesus returns. Hallelujah!

> Being confident of this, that he who began a good work in you will carry it on to completion until the day of Christ Jesus. (NIV)

THY WORD IS A LAMP

The entries in my journals are all personal and real to me. When I sense that I "hear" the Lord speak, it is not a booming voice from the sky but a quiet nudging in my heart. It is an impression, a sense of knowing, a calm believing. The things I sense that I hear from God are for me and no one else. The things you hear from God are for you and not for me. Scripture is God's eternal Word written for all of us. I believe He always speaks to us in His Word and also to each individually when we have need. My journal is a book of my heart cries and God's loving encouragements. I'd like to share a few of those entries with you.

Looking back over my journal in 1980, there is an entry in August that says, "Life is full of problems, Lord." Time doesn't change much, does it? The Lord has told us that fact already in His Word. He has said that in our life in this world, we will have troubles but that He has overcome this world. I often call this a broken world. It was broken in 1980, and it remains broken today.

My next sentence in the journal says, "I'm training you, my child, to handle the future. You will be able to do that in Me." I appreciated that word to my heart from God's Spirit. I do trust that He is always at work in His world and at work in me to be able to handle life. That message brought peace to my heart.

In 1980, there were entries about me wondering if Bill was one day going to be a pastor. He was preparing us both. There were less-weighty issues like me wanting to lose weight and stop biting my fingernails (I still struggle with them both). At that time, I was trying to help teach my children to start their day with a quiet time. Our breakfast around the kitchen bar was often a great opportunity to use a devotional with each of them as we connected with God in the morning.

I wrote entries about Billy and Rick, our foster son, learning to drive and my concern for their safety. I asked the Lord to help me take care of the temple of His Spirit, my body. Consistent exercise was hard for me. I asked God to protect Beth's heart and mind as she grew. I prayed for Bill as he worked, as he coached his wrestling team, as he related to others, as we related to each other as a couple, and as we worked to parent our children. We had successes and failures, but God was ever present and changing us.

I loved to make Scripture personal and pray the prayers His Word held. "I claim Colossians 1:9–12," I wrote, "that I may be filled with the knowledge of Your will in all spiritual wisdom and understanding, so I may walk in a manner worthy of You. Lord, I want to please you in all respects, bearing fruit in every good work and increasing in the knowledge of God. I want to be strengthened with all power, according to Your glorious might, for attaining of all steadfastness and patience, joyously giving thanks to the Father, who has qualified me to share in the inheritance of the saints in light."

In 1981 I said, "Lord, today Your Word seems to be telling me to seek first your kingdom. Help me to see how to seek Your kingdom above all else…to concentrate on the important and not worry about the urgent. Thank You, Jesus." In those days there were so many urgent demands on my time, and I sincerely was trying to sort it all out. As I wrote, He worked His will and His ways into my life.

I am grateful the Lord taught me to journal.

WHAT FILLS YOUR HEART?

> Hear O Israel: The LORD our God, the LORD is one. Love the LORD your God with all your heart and with all your soul and with all your strength.
>
> —Deuteronomy 6:4–5 NIV

This prayer from Deuteronomy is called the Shema. It was the centerpiece of morning and evening Jewish prayer services. It is written in the imperative tense in the Hebrew language, which gives a command, order, request, advice, warning, or instruction. For example, in the imperative one might say, "Listen to me carefully" or "Watch out!" In this scripture, Moses is exhorting God's followers to love God with all their heart, soul, and strength. Jesus underscores this command in Matthew 22:37–40 and adds the word *mind* to the list of ways we are to love God. It seems we are instructed to have unreserved devotion to our God in all areas of our life.

Originally, this passage in the Old Testament was for the Israelites in the wilderness, instructing them to teach their children to have a heart for God. To do that, they, the parents, first had to know God and have a heart for Him themselves. We are further instructed concerning our heart in Psalm 119:2, where it says, "How blessed are those who observe God's testimonies, who seek Him with all their heart" (NAS).

In her book *I Saw the Lord*, Anne Graham Lotz speaks about "having heart." She cites former coach Tom Landry of the Dallas Cowboys as saying, "The difference between a good athlete and a great one is eighteen inches—the distance from the head to the heart." He explained that "good athletes have exceptional ability and a thorough understanding of the game, but great athletes have heart—a passion to play that drives them to selfless sacrifice, brutally long hours of practice, undivided focus and ultimately to achieve extraordinary accomplishments" (Lotz, p 35)

Lotz goes on to say that many Christians she meets are good Christians but few are great ones. She says the difference is the same eighteen inches. While these good Christians have an adequate head knowledge of Scripture, attend worship regularly, and are comfortable with Bible study and prayer, there are few that are great. She says, "There are relatively few Christians who are in love with Jesus."

My Bill loved Jesus. His life in the first twenty-six years was lived as a heathen, he often said. After God captured his heart, he began to grow and learn and change. I can still see him sitting at his old rolltop desk in the big room in our Brush Valley house in Indiana. There were not many days in his redeemed life that he did not start the day with the Lord in God's Word and prayer. His sermons, teachings, and life lessons were forged at that desk.

Bill displayed passion in his wrestling career, and it proved to be a worthy character trait. Having passion, along with a good measure of skill, won him many matches. Over the years, I witnessed how God used passion to form the "new Bill Blacksmith." Passion for Jesus drove him to work tirelessly in his career and coaching years and then to study hard and long at Fuller Seminary. Leading a church as a first-time pastor in his sixties was both difficult and rewarding, and it was fueled by passion. He followed what he believed God was leading him to do with devotion and heart and longed to help others do the same.

OUR FAMILY

Our family has always been very important to both Bill and me. Our first child, William August Blacksmith IV, whom I still call Billy, was born on November 25, 1963. He was named after his father, grandfather, and great-grandfather, which was common in those days. All four generations of William August Blacksmiths were living at that time, which was kind of cool. It was a bit confusing, though, when someone called out "Bill" and all four turned their heads.

Billy is a kind, witty, faithful, and very likeable man. His BS degree is in science, and he is also a guidance counselor. He is a great father to his brood of three boys. Two of these children, Josh and Luke, have special needs. Josh, the eldest, is now in heaven with Bill. Matt is in the middle, and Luke completes their family. Billy has a strong faith in Jesus Christ, and although life is not easy, he has shown that God's grace is sufficient. Bill and Deb have taken the lemons of life and made lemonade. Their story has been a witness to many.

Our second child is Elizabeth Ann Blacksmith, born on January 17, 1972. Beth was a very fun child to parent, very creative, loving, and personable with many friends. Beth took a semester of college to do a Discipleship Training School in Amsterdam with Youth with a Mission. It was a wonderful experience for her, where she was able to make her family's faith her own. She spent three months in Amsterdam and then went to Yugoslavia and Hungary on outreach trips. It was scary to have our nineteen-year-old so far away, but a real blessing in her life.

Beth earned her BS and MA in elementary education with a minor in psychology. She taught first grade before she and Ed started their family. They have three wonderful children, Caleb, Michaela, and Gideon. Beth is creative, loving, generous, and dedicated to her family and fills their lives with many opportunities for growth and fun. She is also a substitute teacher.

It was a hot August day in 1978 when Richard Allen Fleming, coming from foster care, arrived to live with us in Brush Valley. Rick was a shy tall guy who was about to begin his tenth-grade year of school. Rick was always very handy with tools and electronics and especially loved to tinker with his motorcycle. He graduated from United High School and Stevens Trade School in Lancaster, where he studied electronics.

Rick is a talented and creative man. He can build a motorcycle from scratch and repair broken cars or machines. He has patience and can problem-solve well. His wife, Brenda; his daughter, Desire, and her husband, Travis; and their little ones, Tabitha and Maverick, complete Rick's family.

A WRESTLING CHAMPION

I can see God's presence in Bill's life from early on. He was a natural athlete, but not much of a student. He used to say that he went to school for twelve years on his own terms and God gave him twelve more years to get it right. I want you to see the things he accomplished both athletically and academically.

Bill began his wrestling career at Cedar Cliff High School in tenth grade. Coach Bob Craig was a wonderful coach, mentor, and friend and was very proud of his boy Bill. When Bill went to Lock Haven State College (later called university), he had the privilege of wrestling for Coach Hubert Jack and Olympian Gray Simons. He was a four- time Pennsylvania State College champion, a two-time NAIA champion, the Wilkes Tournament champion, and a Division I national champion in 1966.

Bill had a famous move called his sit out, which always amazed fans and opponents who couldn't believe he could get off the bottom so fast. He wrestled all four years of college and ended his senior year with the best win of all. Unable to attend the NCAA tournament at Iowa State, in Ames, Iowa,

Billy and I spent the weekend at my parents' home. A friend at Lock Haven could get the match by radio and called to play the radio broadcast on the phone to my dad and me as we cheered our way long distance through Bill's victory.

Adorning the walls of the field house at Lock Haven are huge posters with pictures of the wrestling heroes of Lock Haven. William August Blacksmith III hangs among them. I am so proud of Bill's wrestling achievements over the years. He was a gifted athlete who had the drive, strength of character, perseverance, and will to win. God had blessed him.

After graduating from Lock Haven in 1966 with a degree in health and physical education, Bill was recruited to come to Indiana University of Pennsylvania as a graduate assistant and to coach the wrestling team. Bill earned his MA in guidance and counseling at IUP in 1968. The head coach decided to retire, and Bill was asked to stay on to coach the team. This was an honor for someone so young, and it was the beginning of our tenure at Indiana, Pennsylvania.

Bill coached for seventeen years and really enjoyed the kids and the whole wrestling scene. A fun fact was that Billy wrestled on Bill's team for the years he went to IUP. He was one of the hardest workers in the wrestling room, and dad and son enjoyed being together on the mat for a season.

In 1985, the Lord provided for Bill to step down from coaching and concentrate on academics. He earned his doctorate in psychology of sport from West Virginia University in 1976, and in 1990 he was promoted to full professor.

One of the greatest memories Bill had at IUP was the "noontime basketball game," which he played for thirty years. The students and faculty played each other, creating wonderful exercise and competition. He was never quite able to duplicate that experience after leaving IUP.

Early retirement was taken in 2002 so that Bill could begin career number 2, full-time ministry. God had built a firm foundation and was continuing to transform us both as we grew to know Jesus better.

VARIOUS TRIALS

Blessed be the God and Father of our Lord Jesus Christ, who according to His great mercy has caused us to be born again to a living hope through the resurrection of Jesus Christ from the dead, to obtain an inheritance which is imperishable and undefiled and will not fade away, reserved in heaven for you, who are protected by the power of God through faith for a salvation ready to be revealed in the last time. In this you greatly rejoice, even though now for a little while you have been distressed by various trials, that the proof of your faith, being more precious than gold which is perishable, even though tested by fire, may be found to result in praise and glory and honor at the revelation of Jesus Christ; and though you have not seen Him, you love Him, and though you do not see Him now, but believe in Him, you greatly rejoice with joy inexpressible and full of glory, obtaining as the outcome of your faith the salvation of your souls.

—1 Peter 1:3–9 NAS

The year was 1974, and we were on vacation in our camper at the beach in New Jersey. One of our favorite treats when we were anywhere near the ocean was steamed clams dipped in melted butter. After one of those yummy dinners, we sat around our picnic table and Bill mentioned that his ankles were swollen and he seemed to be retaining fluid. This was not a common thing, but we thought it might have been a result of too much salt in our "vacation diet." When we got home from our trip, he went to a physician, who gave him a diuretic, and all seemed fine again. In a short time, the swollen ankles returned.

Since Bill's dad was a physician; he ordered some blood work, and Bill was hospitalized in Harrisburg for more tests. The results of the battery of tests were not encouraging. His brother Jim, a medical student, was interning at that time and shared with us that Bill had some sort of kidney disease, and from what they could determine, it was serious. He needed to have a kidney biopsy to further figure this out. Bill was transferred to Hahnemann Hospital in Center City, Philadelphia. Hahnemann was a large academic medical center.

The biopsy was done, but we didn't see the results for three days. During that time, Bill was alone and had a lot of opportunity to think, pray, and reflect on what was happening. He told me the story of how God's Word spoke to his heart during this time. He had been reading his Bible and talking with the Lord, and the scripture from 1 Peter 1:3–9 seemed to pop out at him. He recalled standing in his room, looking out the window and pondering that scripture. There was no air-conditioning in that hospital at that time, but the windows opened, so he was trying to get some fresh air. It was hot, and the air was stagnant, and the sheer window curtains hung limp at his side. He felt like the Lord had spoken to his heart in that "still small voice," assuring him that he was not going to die of this kidney disease but that this whole ordeal would be just "a trial" for him. That was welcome news, but as we all are prone to do, he questioned whether the Lord had spoken, or had he just imagined it? Trying to determine the source of the message, he continued to ask the Lord if it was, indeed, He who spoke. Right then a strong wind blew in his window, billowing the curtains high up toward the ceiling and bringing cool relief to a sweltering evening. The breeze kept up strongly for several minutes, then stopped abruptly, leaving the air and curtains still, as they had been before. Bill had his answer.

God can speak to us in many different ways, but this was at a crucial time when Bill needed God's encouragement. In the midst of our darkest nights, He is there and He cares.

BETHEL COVENANT COMMUNITY

God planted a vision in a group of friends about living together on common ground, in a place where they could commit to one another and serve the Lord together. Bill and I had the privilege of being part of that group. After looking for almost a year for the perfect plot of ground (we had a list of criteria for this "perfect" place), we found a parcel of almost one hundred acres in Brush Valley. It had a pole barn, a massive home, and ninety-three acres of wooded land. After praying and fasting and seeking the Lord's will, we purchased this land and began Bethel Covenant Community

The timing of this coincided with Bill's year in residency at West Virginia University, where he was studying for his doctorate. We had sold our home in Indiana before it ever hit the market, and we packed up all our earthly belongings into three parcels: those things that were headed to graduate school with us, those things that would be left in the Bethel big house for use while we were gone, and those things that were to be put in the attic of the house until we returned. We were planning to share the big house with one of the families eventually, but in the interim, the other two families lived there while they built individual homes on the property.

This adventure of Bethel Covenant Community from approximately 1975 to 1990 was perhaps the hardest and yet the most fruitful time in our lives. It was a catalyst that God used to develop perseverance, patience, love, and joy in us as people. Bethel became a place where others came for picnics, youth retreats, couples' oneness weekends, prayer and praise services, ropes course experiences, and other ministries. We were misunderstood by the neighborhood around us and yet respected as those with strong Christian beliefs.

Our community had eight families at its peak. We had community meetings once a week and prayer and praise on Sunday nights. We went on retreats as a group and even vacationed together. There were disagreements, tears, laughter, and joy as we learned to share and play and live life together. "As iron sharpens iron, so one man sharpens another," Scripture says in Proverbs 27:17 NIV. It was wonderful and awful and great and terrible all at the same time. As God sandpapered off our rough edges, He was changing us each to be more like Jesus.

We had many wonderful parties and celebrations. One particular habit this weird group had was to hide when someone left the room for whatever reason. The individual that left would return to find an empty room, which required them to find everyone who was hiding. Yes, I know, it was childish but oh-so fun. When any of us turned forty, there was a big celebration for the birthday boy or girl. When Bill had his big birthday, the community borrowed a friend's Mercedes car for a day and Bill had the luxury auto that he always wanted, wrapped up in a big red bow. For my fortieth,

I arrived at the event wearing a long skirt to hide the juice-can stilts that Bill had made for me so that I was no longer "Small Hall." Hall was my maiden name.

I am sure that our children especially benefitted from community life. They participated in our prayer and praise services, helped on the ropes course, and served on outreaches, such as programs in nursing homes. I am grateful to the Lord for giving us this unique opportunity to live a portion of our lives with others who shared our love for Him. Difficult circumstances can often be God's plan for His children as He grows their character.

WEST VIRGINIA UNIVERSITY

Bill began his doctoral studies at West Virginia University in the early seventies by taking classes during the summers. We spent two summers in Morgantown, where we house-sat a home in a lovely neighborhood and got involved in service at Trinity Episcopal Church. Although we were members of the Presbyterian Church in Indiana, we sought a church home in Morgantown, not by denomination, but by where God was moving among the people. We found Trinity to be that place. We were young in our faith but wide-eyed and eager to grow and to share the things we were learning with others.

Many institutions of higher learning require that students spend a year in residency, which we did in 1976–1977. During that year, he had to fulfill a variety of duties. He took classes, taught a couple courses for the university, did his research, and wrote his dissertation, all in that twelve-month period. It was a very full year but one filled with new relationships and purposeful living.

My task was to try to keep everyone smiling and to minimize chaos. It was a challenge in such close quarters, but I found some Christian women who were also wives of students. We frequently got together for fellowship and study and to provide a playgroup for our children.

It was not just a change of pace for Bill and me; our children had new experiences as well. Billy attended seventh grade in Morgantown and had to trudge home from school up a steep hill to our new home. We lived in student housing in a tiny two-bedroom apartment with a bath and a kitchen/living room combination. Billy and Beth had to share a bedroom, so we borrowed bunk beds. Beth turned five that year, and both the kids have memories of falling asleep to the tune of the typewriter. It was cozy and hectic at times, but we were on an interesting journey together, and we thrived.

As I think of that time, one interesting memory comes to the forefront. There was a lady, much older than I, who walked around the neighborhood with her native dress. She could have been from the Middle East, but I don't know. I was eager to strike up a conversation with her but soon learned that she did not speak English. She came from time to time and knocked on my door, wanting to come in and do her knitting. It sounds rather absurd now, but I decided to share the gospel with her and see what God would do. She listened, not understanding a word of what I was saying, but nodded and smiled. I will be interested to discover if Suhela is in heaven when I get there. Who knows?

Sometimes dissertation writing takes a very long time. One factor affecting this is the speed of the chairman and of the dissertation committee. If they move in a timely manner, the pieces of the puzzle can be put in place quickly. If not, time slips away and processes are stalled. It was a really interesting period in our lives as we saw the Lord use Bill's major adviser to be a catalyst moving the process along rapidly. Although Bill was really busy, the Lord led us to get involved in various ministries in the church, where we met lifelong friends. People could not believe that Bill could get all that was required of him accomplished in this residency year and still do all the other outreach things he did. But it happened. I am firmly convinced that it went so smoothly because God called us to do some ministry along the way and we tried to be obedient. In Matthew 6:33 it says that we should seek first the kingdom of God and His righteousness and He will take care of the rest of life. We saw it happening as God provided the strength, stamina, and wherewithall to bring the whole thing to completion. Praise be to God!

SHARING THE GOOD NEWS

I always believed I would be a teacher someday. I loved children, and as a young girl, I enjoyed helping out in my church nursery. I would cuddle little people until their parents arrived and play the games they chose and color the pictures they selected. My elected course of study in college was elementary education—what else would it be? My master's was also in elementary education, and my first teaching job was in first grade. I loved it! After Beth was born, I was able to substitute-teach quite a bit, mostly in the primary grades. Life was good!

Then, ever so slowly, my interest changed from instructing little ones to sharing with my peers. My first attempt at teaching a class of adults was in Wednesday-morning ladies' Bible study, where I was asked to teach a series on child discipline. I was pleasantly surprised to be the one selected, and humbled by it all. I labored weeks reading everything I could find on raising and nurturing children and taking copious notes. I realized how much I was enjoying the process as I developed the lessons and filed ideas in neatly stacked folders. My call from the Lord seemed to be changing, and I was enjoying the journey.

Over time I found that I was receiving invitations to speak at other venues: Women's Aglow Fellowship, the elementary school PTA, the local Episcopal church Sunday school class, and one of the ministry groups at my church. At this point, I was still substitute-teaching children, but these occasional opportunities to stand before women to share life was exhilarating. The Lord gave me occasion over the years to generate and teach several Bible studies. One of them is still in existence today under new leadership. It brings a smile to my face.

Bill and I were beginning to do a lot of team-teaching, and I found great satisfaction preparing and presenting lessons from God's Word. It warmed my heart to be able to share some of what God was teaching me and to make application to life alongside others who were seeking to know Him better. We found our very best friends were those in our Sunday school class. We were doing life together, and it was good.

I am waiting to see in what ways the Lord wants me to teach in this new season of life. At first, it was hard for me to have the will to do any new groups without Bill. Gradually, I saw the Lord give me nudges to get with His program. He led me to open up a ladies' life group in my home consisting of longtime friends and new neighborhood acquaintances. I became somewhat "overgrouped" for a time, but it was a lovely season of getting to really know some women I only recognized by name. I was loved on by so many special people. They must have known that this widow needed comfort and community.

I have also felt a desire to be more intentional in sharing with my grandchildren. That is not always easy to do. When I say *intentional,* I am quite serious. Unless it is intentional, it doesn't happen. It is much easier to just have fun with them. Fun is important as well, but I remember Bill being so intentional in his conversations with everyone. I don't want to always be in "instructive mode," but I do want to be aware of where they each are in their life and their walk with Jesus and not miss those divine appointments that He brings to share His good news.

THERE'S NO RETIREMENT
IN THE KINGDOM

In the early eighties, we visited College Hill Presbyterian Church in Cincinnati, Ohio, and heard Dr. Jerry Kirk, pastor, speak on the topic "What are you going to do when you retire?" We were far from retirement at that point, but it was a "God moment" for Bill. Dr. Kirk made the point that there is no retirement in the kingdom of God and that when we are older, have more resources and more time, God still wants to use our gifts to build His kingdom. Bill thought and prayed about that for a long while.

In 1984 and 1985, Bill took two doctor of ministry courses from Fuller Theological Seminary in the summer. They were two-week intensive courses that required a ton of reading outside of class. I was along for the ride but enjoyed doing some of the reading also. We both loved the courses from Fuller and reasoned that seminary would be great.

By this time, I caught the vision and we both felt like God was leading us to prepare for full-time ministry, even though we had many more years before we retired. We searched for East Coast options to attend seminary, but the best place we found was Fuller in Pasadena, California, where we could attend in summers, and each summer equaled a semester. So we enrolled, and off we went to Fuller for summers 1986–1991. To make this financially possible, we house-sat for people in the seminary community when they were away and had no trouble finding homes the whole time we were there. One summer we moved seven times, which was a bit much. Our homes were very diverse, from lovely mansions with pools and guesthouses to small modest homes in multiethnic neighborhoods with feral cats in the backyard and ducks and barking dogs next door. We pet-sat as well and made wonderful friends with Snowy and Pally, two very special dogs.

Billy was in graduate school and teaching and Beth was in eighth grade when we began our journey to Pasadena. Billy obviously could not go with us, and Beth thought it would be great if she were to stay home with her friends and do her cheerleading instead of coming with us. Not! For a couple of those years, she did come out two weeks later than we did so she could be at cheerleading practice, but for the most part, she was with us for the whole time. At first, she was one unhappy camper. But once we settled into Pasadena Four Square Church with Pastor Ralph and Tim as youth director, she had found her niche. We all had. It was a wonderful place to worship and fellowship, and God gave the spiritual fellowship we needed.

I was able to take classes right along with Bill. If we paid for a full load for him, I could take four classes and only pay for one. It was a great deal called team ministry. I was able to choose the classes I wanted and graduated with a master's degree in theology in Christian Formation and Discipleship. Bill's course selection was more structured, but he graduated with a master of divinity, which was required for ordination. He was ordained in 1999 at our home church, Graystone.

We often said that maybe we were at seminary primarily for Beth. She was able to do a mission trip to Mexico with the youth, and during that time she made her faith her own. She graduated from high school in June of 1990 and began studies at IUP right away. She took summer and fall classes and then left for a six-month discipleship training course with YWAM (Youth with a Mission). When she returned in June, we were again in Pasadena.

It is truly amazing how God works in each of us for our good and His glory.

IT'S ALL GREEK TO ME

"Katie has agreed to help me," Bill commented on Saturday morning. "She's a gem. She knows how difficult this is for me."

We had both enrolled in a beginner Greek class offered at Graystone, thinking that it would give us a head start on the upcoming Greek in seminary. The teacher promised that he would take us slowly and teach us only beginner skills. I was actually only doing this for fun as my seminary class plan did not require Greek and I was not going to elect it—not in a million years. I think I attended the church class three times until I felt hopelessly lost and dropped out. Bill hung in there and also enlisted Katie's expert help in conjunction with the class. Katie was a friend who was born and raised in Greece and really gave Bill the head start he needed. She would reinforce the vocabulary and grammar rules right along with the class teacher, and Bill made progress.

When Bill eventually scheduled Greek at Fuller, he attended with a bit of fear and trepidation but ended up doing very well in the course. He reminded me in his humorous way that English often felt like a second language to him.

He not only had to learn the nuances in Greek but also had to learn the English counterpart. I was proud of his tenacity in the quest to learn this difficult language, especially when I had bailed out so quickly.

The Easter after Bill started studying with Katie, he learned an Easter greeting that we often said, but this time it was in Greek. The church, after Jesus' resurrection, would greet one another with the statement, "Christ is risen! He is risen, indeed!"

The Greek translation is "Christos Anesti! Alethos Anesti!"

When I hear that Easter greeting now, my mind and heart go right back to those days of trying to learn and understand a new language. Bill had taught his Sunday school class and the congregation this Greek Easter declaration, and I can see him enthusiastically proclaiming on Easter morning, "Christos Anesti!" to which the gathering of friends would respond, "Alethos Anesti!"

Yes, He is risen! He is risen, indeed! I know I need to remind myself of this truth not only on Easter but every day as well. Life is hard. This is a broken world, and if I fix my gaze on life and its trouble, I will go under. Because He is risen and lives in me, and He promises to never leave me, then I can live in joy and not sorrow, hope and not fear. Why is it that we forget things like this that are so important? I don't know that answer, but I do know that God wants us to get His Word into our minds and hearts so we can live by them. That is our antidote to combat all the lies, negativity, and despair that the world brings.

He is risen! He is risen, indeed!

TEAM MINISTRY

What do you do when you believe God has called you to do something but others do not? What happens when those "others" are the ones who are the "deciders"? And what if there is the distinct possibility that you are wrong and have made a mistake? What do you do?

Years ago, Bill and I found ourselves, little by little, planning, teaching, and facilitating ministries together. It was not something we had deliberately tried to do. It just seemed to happen. In many ways it was a harder way to operate than just one of us making the decisions. Coordination is never easy, but there it was. Team Ministry!

A position opened up in the church we were serving to be director of adult ministry. We were already doing much of what was required in the job description, so it seemed quite natural for us to apply as a team. We knew that having two people do one job might be a bit different from the ordinary, so we did not take the application task lightly. We prayed individually about this often, and in the days ahead of the deadline, we set aside a day of prayer and fasting to continue to seek what God wanted. Although we both did this, we did not do it together. We went separate ways for the day with Bible, tablet, and pen in hand and with the expectation that we would meet back together in the evening and discuss what we thought the Lord wanted us to do.

What a special time it is to sit at the Lord's feet like Mary, the sister of Martha and Lazarus in the Bible. As a busy person, I understand how hard it is to find a quiet place and an extended time to do this. What a blessing it is to enjoy His presence without the pressure to move on and do the next thing but instead to do the better thing.

When Bill and I met back together that evening, we determined that we both felt the answer was yes, we were to apply for the position as a team. We did that and waited eagerly for the verdict. The call came the next week that the "deciders" were impressed with our résumé and were ready to hire one of us.

But you don't understand, I thought. *We function as a team, and that is how we want to do this ministry.* The decision had been made, and "we" were not hired. It was disappointing to say the least. Where had we gone wrong? Had our "spiritual ears and heart" heard Him wrong? I found myself in a miry pit of hurt and questioning the Lord about my ability to hear *anything* He had to say. It was hard to move forward, but we had to move forward, so we continued life and the Lord continued to work.

About eight years later, we were recognized as a team ministry and became codirectors of spiritual formation and discipleship. I learned that sometimes God's leading is not for the present time but for a time that is yet to come. I also learned that even when we make mistakes and think we don't hear God, He continues to work and picks us up and sets us on level ground. Whether we hear correctly or not, He wants to speak to us and will continue to do so. Our task is to sit at His feet and learn.

THE WISDOM OF ROCKY

"You like her?" Paulie questions.

"I dunno. She's got gaps, I've got gaps, together we fill gaps," Rocky Balboa declares to his brother-in-law, Paulie, during their conversation about Rocky's wife, Adrian, from the movie *Rocky*.

I love this exchange. Being married to Bill Blacksmith meant that I heard it multiple times as we had watched all the Rocky movies more than once. I probably wouldn't hold up Rocky as the epitome of wisdom, but he got it right on this one.

As I've mentioned before, Bill and I were a team. God prepared us and trained us to teach together, and we served an adult Sunday school class for years. People were always asking how long we had to practice to weave our comments together. We did not practice; we just did it. Bill was the lead teacher, and when he came to a spot in the lesson where I had a comment, I would jump in. I did ask him once during our Saturday-morning individual preparation if it was hard for him when I did that and if it broke his focus.

His response was, "Heck no! It gives me a chance to take a breath and regroup as I gather my thoughts. I'm glad when you bring your ideas into the lesson."

We got comfortable enough with the plan that if either of us began to share something at an inopportune time, we would say, "Could you hold that thought while I finish this idea?"

Bill and I each had "gaps"—lots of them. I'm lacking the gene that helps with directionality. Bill, on the other hand, was great at that. If we were at the grocery store together or at a mall, my "modus operandi" was to exit the building and go the exact opposite way from the one to our car. My thoughtful husband often would whisper "Go left" or "Go right" as we walked into the parking lot. He had inherited that special gene and only had to visit a destination once, and he was all set to go there again twenty years later. Not me, man! I had trouble even following maps. So glad someone invented the GPS.

One of Bill's greatest challenges was remembering someone's name. He did well with faces but really struggled with names. That is a huge deficit for a pastor to have. When I could, I would stand before him in a greeting line and mention the person's name before he had to greet them. Names came easily for me.

Bill had gaps, Linda had gaps, and together we filled gaps.

WORSHIP AND SERVICE

We moved to Indiana, Pennsylvania, in 1966 and joined Graystone Church in 1969. Many memories were forged at Graystone—Marriage Made Marvelous, Alpha, small groups, Summer's Best Two Weeks; men and women's ministries and events; Prime Time and TNT Sunday school classes, to name a few. Graystone was our home, and we made forever friends during those years.

Bill retired from IUP in June 2002, and we kept our eyes and ears open to discover what God had for us in this new season of life. In January 2004, we left Graystone to seek the Lord's direction for full-time ministry. They gave us a very meaningful going-away party that I will never forget.

Bill accepted a call to be senior pastor of Highland Presbyterian Church in New Castle in January 2005, and we began ministry in there in February. Highland is a lovely old Presbyterian Church in a changing neighborhood. An office was created for me, and I became the pastoral assistant with oversight of the staff and of spiritual formation. Bill did a marvelous job of loving the people, presiding over session meetings, preaching engaging and practical sermons, casting vision for the future, and increasing the membership. He was loved and respected, and God used him in great ways during those five years. During that time, we made many lifelong friends.

After leaving Highland, we were invited to join the staff of Grace Chapel Community Church in Hermitage to serve in the life group ministry. Life groups were like Bible studies but more. They were places where people can grow in faith, serve others, and live life together with friends. We served the people of Grace Chapel from October 2010 until retiring for the third time in the spring of 2014. Our time at Grace Chapel was full of wonderful people and new ministry opportunities. We learned much about life groups and their importance in our faith walk and were able to experience ministry in a large and growing congregation. It was exhilarating to help men and women plug into a group of new friends as they became a part of the Grace Chapel family.

When we were sixty, we decided that when Bill turned seventy, we would slow down and move back to Indiana, Pennsylvania, to be closer to our children and grandchildren. That move happened in the fall of 2014, and we downsized and settled in a condo just outside of town. It was a good move for us as we were now close enough to visit our kids and see the grandchildren's events and sports.

"There is no retirement in the kingdom" was still very much a part of our DNA, but now we were in a new season of life and not really knowing how God wanted to use us. We prayed a lot about that as we tried to follow His lead.

WHAT'S THE "THEREFORE" THERE FOR?

A comment that people make to me goes something like this: "Today I heard an expression that Bill often said" or "I remember Bill saying that" or "Bill always used that phrase."

This happens a lot, and I love it. I hardly think anyone would be able to remember or even want to remember anything I have said over the years. But with Bill, people do want to remember. He taught with such passion, humor, and clarity that his phrases and words were memorable. As I look back and reflect on those phrases, hearing his words again in my memory is very healing.

So often in Scripture you run into the word *therefore*. There are over one thousand listings of the word *therefore* in the concordance. It is important to know what this means if you want to understand the passage in question. Bill often shared that question with the adults he was teaching. He would ask,

"And what is the *therefore* there for?"

When we see *therefore*, we need to back up a paragraph or two and see what was being said before the word *there-*

fore. When we understand the context of the story, the next part makes better sense. Because of *this,* then we can say *this.* Because of what was just said, the consequences are this. This is how the dots are connected. For that reason, this is so.

For instance, in Deuteronomy 29:27 it says,

"Therefore, the LORD's anger burned against this land, so that he brought on it all the curses written in this book" (NIV).

So why was the Lord upset with the people? We have to go back to verse 26 and even before that to see

"They went off and worshiped other gods and bowed down to them, gods they did not know, gods he had not given them" (NIV).

It is an easy concept, but so often we just skip over it without fully understanding why the word is used. It was important to Bill to understand the context of what he was reading in Scripture. I will forever take notice when the word *therefore* is used.

He taught me well.

THY WORD HAVE I HID
IN MY HEART

I would love to have a dollar for every conference, class, teaching event, or seminar that we have attended over the years—well, maybe ten dollars for each would be better.

One of the challenges of gaining new thoughts and ideas that are received at an event is putting these new learnings into practice. Application. I often find myself being so inspired during the course of the event that I write it down in a notebook as I scurry to catch each nugget, then file the notebook neatly away on my bookshelf, never to be opened again. Oh, I am sure my heart and mind have captured a remnant of the gems that I've heard, but like a leaky faucet, drop by drop, I seem to lose what I have stored away in my head and my abandoned notebook.

Bill had a better way of ensuring that he would remember nuggets of wisdom. He wrote within the margins of his Bible. Not only did he take notes on paper like I did, but he would also summarize the gems he didn't want to forget where he would see them again and again, right beside the scripture to which they referred. His Bible is a treasure chest. Bill read through the Bible several times a year using the Chronological Bible and also had various versions of Scripture that he used in his quiet time. For many years, the New American Standard was his favorite, then the New International Version, and more recently the English Standard Version. He found it helpful to read the Word in different versions, but his favorite "teaching Bible" was his NIV Life Application Bible.

This particular book of his has become a prize possession to me in this season of life without him. It is full—and I use that term literally—full of notes, words, illustrations, Post-It Notes, etc. on nearly every page. I wish he were here physically so I could ask him about some of his thoughts and notations. He would also write when he heard that "still small voice" of Jesus as he studied the Word. Those intimate, private words are so precious to me now. Some I do not understand, and probably they are not meant to be understood on this side of eternity. Oh, I wish I could sit and talk with him for a while.

This teaching Bible was with Bill in Fuller Seminary as we house-sat and dog-sat. The fully taped cover and binding of the Bible remind me of the dog Snowy and his canine desire to "feast upon the Word." So much would have been lost if Bill had discarded that Bible, so he cocooned it in clear tape, and voilà, all is well.

Bill's prayer list was attached to his pocket calendar and written in such small print that I need a magnifying glass to read it. He always printed small. That skill allowed him to be able to really use the margins of his Bible fully. Some of the names on his list are written in red ink. I guess they were people in *real* need of prayer.

Some of my most precious memories are of Bill sitting at his beautiful old rolltop desk with his mind and heart deep in thought as he met daily with the Lord in God's Word. He was the one who taught me the importance of regular, daily meetings with God and what a relationship with Jesus looked like. "I have hidden your word in my heart that I might not sin against you" (Ps. 119:11 NIV).

THE DAYS OF DIALYSIS

After Bill's kidneys had deteriorated to a point that he felt sick and had dangerously high blood values, he was given the choice of what kind of dialysis he wanted to do. *Hemodialysis* is where the body's blood is pumped through an artificial kidney that filters it and then pumps the blood back into the body. *Peritoneal dialysis* is where a fluid is fed by gravity into the peritoneum, the cavity of the abdomen that is around the organs, and the poisons that the kidneys don't filter out are drawn into the fluid and then discarded. He chose the process that was gentler on the body, peritoneal dialysis. The only prerequisite was that the patient be fastidious, and I knew Bill could do it.

In this type of dialysis, the fluid would go from its bag on an IV pole into the catheter and into Bill's body. After the fluid had been in his body for a few hours, then it was drained out and new fluid put in. Bill began peritoneal dialysis in the fall of 1995. But first, he had to have a Tenckhoff catheter positioned in his abdomen to allow the fluid a place to enter. The first catheter did not work, so it had to be removed, and another inserted. This was a surgical procedure and required hospitalization and a healing period each time.

The little chorus that we used to sing at prayer and praise at Bethel was running through my mind over and over as we were in our doctor's dialysis clinic at UPMC. We were testing out the second Tenckhoff catheter for Bill's peritoneal dialysis debut.

> Rejoice evermore, for this is the will of God.
> Pray without ceasing, for this is the will of God.
> In everything give thanks, for this is the will of God,
> In Christ Jesus concerning you.

This song is taken from Scripture in 1 Thessalonians 5:16, which says, "Be joyful always; pray continually; give thanks in all circumstances, for this is God's will for you in Christ Jesus" (NIV).

As we began the process, we sat in an examination room, praying that this time it would work. Nothing happened for what seemed like forever. It was suggested that perhaps we should walk around a bit, so we did, Bill pushing the IV pole in front of him as we both circled the halls around and around.

This song kept reminding me that in everything I was supposed to give thanks. In everything, not just when things were hunky-dory, but even when things weren't! I have heard it said that we are to thank God *for* everything. I'm not sure He is encouraging me to thank Him that Tenckhoff catheters don't work, but I am sure He wants me to thank Him in the midst of life whether the catheter works or not. I believe He is saying, "Trust me, my beloved, in this trial of life. Learn what it means to put your full weight on Me even when you feel weak and defeated. I am strong, and I will work this out."

Little by little that day, the catheter began to function and peritoneal dialysis became Bill's four-times-a-day ritual for ten months. He would do this dialysis at his desk at home in the morning, at his desk at work at lunch, at home during dinner, and then before bed. It required a person to be extraordinarily careful and supermeticulous so that infection would not result. Bill maintained a clean bill of health throughout the process.

The fluid came in big bags that he attached to an IV pole at home and at work. A big truck delivered monthly supplies to our home, and we stored them in the heated garage at Bethel. The fluid needed to be warmed a bit so as not to be too cold when it went inside the body. Thank God for microwaves!

It sounds like a tedious process, and it was, but Bill kept working at IUP during these ten months of dialysis and even played ice hockey. Can you believe? He had a protective shell that one of his IUP colleagues made him, and he used it while playing sports to prevent injury to the dialysis site and, even after he received a new kidney, to protect the surgery site. I know I would have been a bit irritated myself to have this life complication, but he did not complain or become depressed about it. He trusted the Lord and kept on with life. It was a little bump in the road to him.

Bill just adjusted his life to include dialysis. If we were camping, we carried along four bags of fluid for each day we were gone. You do what you have to do, and Bill was a real trooper during this process. Even when life is hard, you can still make the adjustments that are needed and enjoy the life that God has given to you. I have seen people just fold up and give up when life throws them a curveball. Not Bill. He made the necessary adjustments without missing a beat. He was grateful that God had given him life.

God does not always answer our prayers the way we want, but He has a plan, and He is sovereign and He is good.

THE HALVERSON BENEDICTION

The Reverend Richard C. Halverson was a pastor for many years, was an author of fourteen books, and served as chaplain of the United States Senate from 1981 to 1994. Sometime in our younger years, we had heard him speak at a Sunday outdoor service during our vacation in Cape May, New Jersey. Once in a great while, one experiences something that profoundly affects one's life thereafter. Hearing Dr. Halverson speak was one of those times. It felt like an anointed moment.

Years later, Bill discovered what has come to be called the Halverson benediction. Dr. Halverson typically used the same benediction to conclude his church services each Sunday. Bill liked it so well he began to use it often to end his services, also.

A benediction is sometimes called a charge or a blessing given at the end of a church service to send the parishioners on their way. It is often little more than wishing the congregation to "have a great week." Dr. Halverson was asked what he felt was the most significant thing he ever shared with his church, and he said it was his benediction.

> You go nowhere by accident.
> Wherever you go,
> God is sending you.
> Wherever you are,
> God has put you there.
> God has a purpose
> in your being there.
> Christ lives in you
> and has something
> he wants to do
> through you where you are.
> Believe this and go in the
> grace and love and
> power of Jesus Christ. (Reverend Richard Halverson)

ROBE OF RIGHTEOUSNESS

God made him who had no sin to be sin for us, so that in him we might become the righteousness of God.

—2 Corinthians 5:21 NIV

For He has clothed me with garments of salvation and arrayed me in a robe of righteousness.

—Isaiah 61:10 NIV

In Wednesday-morning ladies' Bible study, we often sang a song about the robe of righteousness. The words are etched in my memory although I don't know who wrote them.

> I am covered over with the robe of righteousness that
> Jesus gives to me, gives to me;
> I am covered over with the precious blood of Jesus,
> and He lives in me, lives in me;
> What a joy it is to know my heavenly Father loves
> me so, He gives to me, my Jesus.

When he looks at me, He sees not what I used to
be but He sees Jesus.

That song brings to mind one Sunday morning at Highland Presbyterian Church when Bill was preaching on what Jesus has done for us. His friend Dennis was sitting in the third row back that morning, dressed in old jeans and a dirty and torn flannel shirt. This was not typical attire for Dennis, but he had been enlisted prior to that day to play a part in the service. Bill taught us that when we put our trust in Jesus and invite Him to sit on the throne of our heart, an exchange takes place. We give him our sin, our filthy rags, and He gives us His robe of righteousness. He gives us His right standing with the Father, His holiness, His nature, and He takes on our sinful nature, our darkness, our despair. Without Jesus we can never come to the Father. We have only filthy rags to offer.

Bill borrowed a visual lesson he had seen Dr. Ron Rand use and came down from the pulpit toward Dennis. He asked Dennis to stand up and slip off his dirty flannel shirt. Bill then took off the white robe he was wearing and placed it on Dennis's shoulders and picked up the dirty shirt. It was a solemn moment as we all understood the object lesson.

Bill preached these words that morning: "The Prophet Isaiah wrote seven hundred years before the birth of Christ, 'But he was pierced for our transgressions and he was crushed for our iniquities; the punishment that brought us peace was upon him and by his wounds we are healed'" (Isa. 53:5 NIV).

He continued, "Christ took our sin and gave us His righteousness, His robe of righteousness. It means to be properly restored, just as if we never sinned. Christ takes our sin, our filthy rags, and gives us His forgiveness, His wholeness, His righteousness, His restoration, His love and peace. He offers it to us as a free gift by His grace."

What a joy it is to know my heavenly Father loves me so!

YOU'VE GOT TO THINK QUICKLY ON YOUR FEET

The communion table was set perfectly. The committee did a good job. The white cloth was ironed and laid evenly on the long mahogany table. I was seated in my regular spot on the front row. I loved seeing Bill in his white robe sharing with the congregation the words of Scripture as we prepared our hearts to participate in communion. He carefully held up the bread and wine (we use juice), reminding us that Jesus is the giver of all life and as we receive these elements we remember what He did for us.

The bread and juice represent Jesus' body and blood. They were served to us by elders as we either remained seated in our pew or as we came forward. This latter method is called intinction. This particular Sunday, we were coming forward. Each person was given a small piece of bread, and they would dip it in the cup of juice. This was a solemn time as we were encouraged to remember Jesus' sacrifice for us on the cross. He died for my sin and rebellion, and as I accept what Jesus did for me, I become his daughter. This meal was a family meal for the children of God gathered and remembering together.

Bill and I had brought a chalice and pitcher with us when we came to Highland Church. I remember the day I bought it at the pottery sale at IUP. Twice a year, the pottery class would hold a public sale for the community to come and purchase items the students had made. This cup and pitcher had a lovely blue-and-brown swirled pattern, which made them especially attractive. They looked beautiful as they sat on the table ready to be used in worship.

During the words of preparation, Bill showed us the bread and the cup and called us to reflect and remember. Because I had listened to my pastors prepare their flock to receive communion all my life, I was familiar with the liturgy. On this particular day, Bill was speaking familiar words, but his actions were different. He had added something unfamiliar. During his explanation of the cup, he poured some of the juice from the pitcher into the chalice as he normally did but then poured out some of the juice into another receptacle before he invited the congregation to come forward. He didn't miss a beat.

Women, men, and some older children filed toward the front, taking the bread and dipping it in the cup. We worshipped in song during the communion process and then ended with a prayer. As the service concluded, Bill and I greeted parishioners at the door as they departed. It was a very meaningful service.

That afternoon, as we were relaxing and discussing the events of the morning, I said, "What was that extra thing you did during communion? Why did you pour out some of the juice once you poured it into the cup? I never saw you do that before."

"Well," Bill slowly answered my question with a grin on his face, "there was a dead fly in the chalice and I needed to get it out of there before people came up for communion."

As I think of that morning now, I can only say, "Wow, way to go, honey! You really thought quickly on your feet."

EGG TIMER AND
THREE CHAPTERS

My living room walls were freshly painted, thanks to granddaughter Michaela, and I had moved the furniture around a bit. *The living room looks bigger and more open,* I thought as I put my decorations back on the bookcase shelf. One of those items was a tall hourglass. It was given to us by Verna and Jim after one of our life group meetings at Grace Chapel. I think it took an hour to empty from one half of the glass to the other as it was turned back and forth, thus the reason it's called hourglass, I guess.

It was a lovely present, but you might wonder why this unusual token was given. It was an enlarged reminder of the small three-minute egg timer that Bill used in our group when he talked about having a quiet time. Christians everywhere along the maturity spectrum are encouraged to meet with God each day in what is sometimes called a quiet time. It is not a special formula to be followed at a prescribed time, place, and length but an open-ended appointment with the living God to hear from Him in His Word, the Holy Scriptures, and to talk with Him in prayer. The purpose is to learn, grow, and get to know our Father better.

Of all the spiritual disciplines, this one is the hardest, I think, to develop and maintain. We all want to connect with the Lord, but life gets busy and noisy and our quiet times seem to fade into the background. One particular life group meeting, Bill was encouraging our members to develop prayer as part of our daily time with God. As a physical reminder, he gave us each a small three-minute egg timer. He shared that in the beginning of our walk with the Lord, an egg timer is a good tool. Turn it over and begin to have a conversation with God. It soon becomes apparent that three minutes is not long enough to share our praises, concerns, requests, or confessions with God. It is a good object lesson and hopefully propels us into longer prayer times.

Another friend, Lisle, was instrumental in our early days of walking with Jesus. He taught us that before his head hit the pillow each night, if he had not already read three chapters of his Bible sometime during that day, he promised the Lord that he would get up and read before he went to sleep. That story became a great reminder of the importance of reading God's Word every day. Early in Bill's walk, he discovered that Psalms 1, 2, and 3 were fairly short, and he had to resort to reading them by default on occasion.

The egg timer and three-chapter rule were prompts, reminders, visuals that meeting with God each day is a crucial step in developing a relationship with Him. We would never think that we could have a relationship with a spouse, a best friend, or our child without time together.

Over the years, I have discovered that I can't live victoriously and grow as a Christian without my time with the

Lord. The time of day, length, place, and content of this appointment can change with situations and seasons of life, but the very act of keeping this meeting daily is a discipline that I have learned to treasure.

WHOSE PAGER IS BEEPING?

"Wasn't the worship wonderful tonight?" Duane reflected as we walked out of the church toward our cars.

"I loved the sermon on Lordship that Pastor Joseph shared," Joyce stated. "It was just what I needed to hear."

It was a hot, humid August evening in downtown Pittsburgh, and a group of us from Graystone was attending a church service. We had caravanned, and our cars were parked several blocks away. It was dark by now, but we were leisurely strolling along when someone's beeper went off. Heads turned back and forth as we tried to determine the source of the sound.

To Bill's dismay, it was his. He had never heard it beep before because it was a very special pager that was given to him by the hospital so they could call him when a kidney became available. The beeper listed a phone number that he was to call immediately. In those days, 1996, we did not own cell phones. For a few minutes we were a bit frazzled, until Marian produced a phone she had and we were able to call the number, get instructions of what to do, and set out for the hospital.

How exciting and how terrifying it was! A kidney was at the University of Pittsburgh Medical Center, waiting for Bill to arrive. Several of our group hugged us, promising to pray through the night, and headed home. Others drove with us to the hospital, and some stayed with me through the night.

As soon as we got there, Bill and I met with the doctors and were told about the procedure and asked if we wanted to receive the kidney. Organs were matched with recipients by blood markers called antigens. Simply stated, this kidney was a three-out-of-six antigen match for Bill. For many years after this, we made the assumption that this kidney was only half as good a match as it could have been for Bill, but we said yes to it anyway. As we prayed and asked the Lord to guide us, we felt like it was the right kidney for Bill. Only recently did we find out that a three-antigen match is like a sibling would have, a very good match. Bill never experienced rejection, and his kidney served him well for twenty-one years.

From 2:00 a.m. until about 7:00 a.m. on August 8, 1996, Bill was receiving this new kidney. The cadaver was a twenty-seven-year old male from Florida who had lost his life in a motorcycle accident. The donated organ had been on ice for over thirty hours.

"The next few days were very difficult—pain, new meds with side effects, lack of sleep, nausea, thirst. Lord, how Bill needs Your ministry," my journal entry read.

The kidney had injury from being on ice for so long, so it needed to heal. It did not cleanse Bill's blood at first. It wasn't working! Gradually, over the next few weeks, it did begin to work and Bill's blood chemistries lowered to a good level.

God spoke to us each during this stressful time. Bill's verse of comfort was from Exodus 19:4b, which said, "I carried you on eagles' wings and brought you to myself" (NIV). My verse was from Deuteronomy 33:27b, "And underneath are the everlasting arms" (NIV).

God cares for His children and brings peace to their hearts, especially in difficult times.

LIFE WITH A NEW KIDNEY

Added to our already-full lives were medications, catheters, occasional IVs, infections, and a whole pile of reasons to trust in the Lord. Bill's new kidney was functioning well, but we found out that with it came a virus that he did not originally have but now did. In the general population, some test positive for CMV and some test negative. Bill was negative, and the kidney was positive. Every time the virus would rear its ugly head, it required an IV course of antibiotics for several weeks. We learned to keep the IV pole handy, and I became good at medical procedures that I never wanted to learn.

I remember during the pretransplant phase, I had to give Bill shots. This may not be a big deal for you, but for me it was monumental. As long as I can remember, I have been terrified of needles, blood, and shots. Blood tests were a major ordeal for me, and I often fainted at the mention of any of the above terms. I can still feel the embarrassment I felt in junior high as I slumped over in the choir loft just "thinking" about an upcoming blood test. In chemistry class in high school, we were learning about lab safety and the teacher graphically talked about a student who was cut with a broken beaker. You can guess what happened to me!

So here I was, wanting to help Bill but fighting my own demons in the process. I practiced giving the shot to an orange. I got so I could do that without much drama. Bill patiently endured my novice nursing, and I got the shot in the right place on his arm almost always. Once, it went in crooked and I nearly lost my lunch, but he said kindly that it was fine.

Urinary tract infections were our enemy. A handful of times, Bill ended up in the hospital at Pittsburgh, being treated with strong drugs and sent home with a PICC line near his heart. So much for not liking needles and blood. The Lord was delivering me from fear by giving me practice as I helped my beloved.

Bill was so grateful for his transplant despite all the trials he went through and would continue to face. I was so impressed that he remained so positive, even in the worst of times. We were faithful to pray for the new kidney to work well, for Bill's body to heal, and for the kidney to last for a long time. God invites us to share our heart with Him, and he encourages us to ask what we will. We did that. He provided peace, comfort, healing, and joy in the process.

I think Christians sometimes believe that God should say yes to all our prayers. He does not. He answers "Yes," "No," and sometimes "Wait." God always hears our requests, and He is a faithful God who loves us, but His plan is not always our plan. His thoughts are way above my thoughts. I have learned to trust Him, most of the time, because He is good and He loves me even when things go wrong.

Bill had said he thought his kidney would last for at least thirty-five years. It lasted for twenty-one years, and his body never rejected the new organ. Pretty cool. At the end, Bill didn't die from kidney failure. That special kidney was holding out strong and mighty. I can see Bill's smile as I say that. He lost his physical battle as a result of autoimmune hemolytic anemia, a blood issue where his body was attacking his own red blood cells. Unexpected and unwanted. That kidney might indeed have lasted thirty-five years.

ALL IDEAS ARE NOT CREATED EQUAL

Living in the culture we do requires discernment. On many occasions, I have clicked on a Netflix movie to find it was way too raunchy to watch. As a couple, Bill and I had decided that we just were not going to watch R-rated movies. That decision was not too hard until we found that many PG-13 flicks should have been Rs and our money at the theater was wasted as we walked out. Then there was the occasional R that was a really good movie if you could ignore the bad words. That's not a good plan either. Can we all agree that finding a good story told in an appropriate way is a hard task?

Bill loved action movies. Me, not so much. He discovered something that seemed to be a great answer to the problem of watching one of his shoot-'em-up shows but avoiding all the bad language. In those days, the movies on TV had bad words bleeped out or silenced so you could record the program on a VHS tape and have a benign rendition to rewatch at a later date. Things were wonderfully arranged, or so we thought! It was legal to do this, and we were excited. When the grandchildren came to visit in succeeding years, Bill could share *Rambo* and *Rocky* with them with no offense.

Well, there was a ramification to this plan that was never foreseen. After a weekend visit with Grami and Papa, the teenaged boys Matthew and Caleb would love to go to school and brag to their friends that they indeed had seen *Rambo* at their Papa's home. Not a good thing on several levels. They forgot to share that the VHS tapes had the bad language deleted and they were getting the Disney version of the movie. So there is a whole generation of parents out there that think we showed our grandkids inappropriate movies. Parents, please hear this disclaimer as of now: We did not! Unless the violence of *Rambo* is a problem. Oh, gosh!

You know, there are friends who have good discernment and judgment and you have learned to trust their wisdom when it comes to the appropriateness of movies. Of course, there are those who you do not trust in this department. We had always prided ourselves as being the parents with good judgment.

And the story continues. One of our Sunday school friends, Maxine, was looking for a movie she and her family could watch together, and she asked Bill for a suggestion. Again, TV and VCR came to the rescue, or so we thought. One of our recent recorded flicks was *My Cousin Vinny*. We had it in the archives of our recorded programs and suggested this family watch it. They decided to watch it on TV rather than borrow our older copy. You can guess what happened.

"Bill Blacksmith, I can't believe you recommended that movie. It was awful!" our friend shared as Bill and I discovered, for the first time, that our fun movie was really rated R and was indeed awful.

With downcast eyes and back a bit slumped, Bill tried to redeem himself by telling her what had happened. So much for sharing our ten-year-old copies of movies. We found we had to be extracareful how we talked about titles from that point on. TV movies in recent years do not bleep out vulgarities. Discovering fun, exciting, and wholesome entertainment these days is a real challenge.

WHAT I APPRECIATE ABOUT YOU

One of the exercises we did with couples that attended our Oneness Weekends at Bethel or our Marriage Made Marvelous events at Graystone was to ask them to list ten things about their spouse that they valued. They would individually write those things on a card and then have a time of sharing what they wrote with their mates. It was good for these couples to reflect on positive qualities that they identified in each other. Those lists were very edifying and helped the men and women remember why they chose each other in the first place.

I have a laminated card in my Bible that Bill wrote to me after doing one of these exercises years ago. I wish it had a date on it. He often told me things he loved about me, and it is so special now to read that card and remember. I'm somewhat of a hoarder. I keep a lot of things. I'm so glad this is one of those things I kept and even laminated to preserve it.

Affirmations of our spouses should not be for retreats only. When was the last time you commented on how grateful you are that he takes care of maintaining the car or how much you enjoy the great meals she prepares? Wouldn't he love to hear you thank him for bringing the paper to you as you finally sit down in the evening? She would certainly love knowing that you valued her hard work at the office! It costs so little to be generous with our praise.

I believe God wants us to affirm not only our spouses but all those He puts in our lives as well. Why is it easier to find fault and be critical of others instead of pointing out to them the positive things we see in them? I think maybe we have to train our minds and hearts to look for the positive in others rather than what we might want to change in them. It probably does not come naturally for us. Discipline rarely does.

Hebrews 10:24 encourages us to "spur one another on toward love and good deeds" (NIV). When we affirm a good quality in someone, we are really lifting up that character trait and helping that brother or sister to see its value and its good effect on us. In that way, he or she might be encouraged to repeat that act.

Every time I read that list of things Bill appreciated in me, it helps me stand a bit taller (which is a feat in and of itself for me since I am very short) and to rise a bit above the brokenness of life. Too much in this life tears us down. Let's be people who look for ways to encourage others and spur them on to build them up rather than tear them down.

RIVIERA MAYA

We discovered Apple all-inclusive vacations somewhere along our journey and thoroughly enjoyed them. Our trip of choice was Mexico's Riviera Maya. The perk of choosing an all-inclusive vacation is that you have no surprises. The tab is calculated up front, and everything is paid for ahead of time. If we were patient and watched for bargains, this could be done very economically. We enjoyed this break from the action and planned several of these getaway times during our life together.

Reflections from Riviera Maya include towels that were formed into animal shapes by the custodial staff, lovely gardens in which to walk, yummy buffets, romantic dinners served in specialty restaurants overlooking the ocean, dancing to a band that came year after year and played our oldies, and participation in many beach volleyball games.

Being the nonathlete of the two of us, I always had a book in hand as I chose a beach chair along the water. I tried to find one close to the volleyball court but not so close as to put me in danger from an errant ball. The weather was forever beautiful, with warm breezes and hot sand, and I loved it. Bill, on the other hand, immediately scoped the landscape for a beach volleyball game that was taking place. He often found himself playing beside men and women who didn't speak English. It amazed me how they could maintain a game without understanding one another, but I guess sport is a universal language. I would read and watch, watch and read. It was a lovely way to spend an afternoon. Bill would play, work up a sweat, and then take a break, but not for long. He loved sports, all sports, and was usually excellent at them all. I was happy as a clam to read and sunbathe.

One year there was a volleyball tournament where the winners were honored by being awarded T-shirts and tequila at the gathering for the evening show. The Red Team, as they were labeled, were summoned up onstage to claim their prizes and high-five each other. What fun to see athletes from various cultures enjoy the camaraderie and celebration without a common language.

I'm grateful Bill and I made the effort and had the resources to take this time away together. This was not a family vacation but a set-aside moment in life for us to be alone, just the two of us. We deliberately tried to build memories as a couple because we knew that life itself had a way of separating married folks. There is a season where our careers, our children, our lives, and our responsibilities take up the majority of our time, but there will come a place on the calendar when the kids grow up and leave and the empty nesters are alone. Some couples find that when that time comes, they are living with a stranger. We deliberately built together time into our schedules all along the way. There was always a weekly date night. It could be as simple as walking to get ice cream or hot dogs by candlelight after kids went to bed or a fancy dinner out. Friday nights now are tough sometimes.

I think Bill was the main driver in this quest for us to build an intimate couple life. It took work and planning, but it was so worth the cost. I am grateful for his creativity, love of life, playfulness, passion, and wisdom, because he led us into a "oneness" that I now appreciate more than ever. If husbands and wives do not prioritize time alone together, life will naturally not provide it.

WE NEED A TRANSLATOR!

When we were away from home, we generally tried to attend worship somewhere on Sundays. It didn't always work, but we gave it the old college try anyway. On one of our visits to Riviera Maya, we met a gentleman while walking on the beach, and in our conversation with him, we learned he was a Christian and attended a church in a little town not far from our resort. When Christian "brothers and sisters" get started talking about the Lord, you never know what will happen.

Carlos invited us to join him on Sunday to go to his small Spanish-speaking church. We obviously did not have a car, but he said not to worry, that he would pick us up and take us with him. Even writing that now makes me shiver a bit. If that happened today, I might be much less inclined to follow through than we were then. I think the world has gotten more dangerous. Nevertheless, the plans were made, and we were all set to meet him at the main entrance to the resort at nine thirty on Sunday. He even indicated that perhaps Bill might want to share something with the congregation. What? Going to a Spanish worship service would be cool, but speaking there? Not sure about that. Bill could speak a bit of German, and I could remember *un petit peu* of French from our high school days, but we had never studied Spanish.

Sunday came, and we were excited about this new adventure. We were wondering how the Lord would work this out. Carlos arrived exactly as he said he would, and we were off to parts unknown in Mexico. Would we ever get back alive? Was he who he said he was, or was he a drug lord? As we arrived, we saw a small adobe structure with a cross on the roof. No question that this building was a church. I was feeling better.

We entered and could sense the many sets of eyes checking us out. There were men in casual white shirts and women in lovely, colorful dresses. Many little children ran around the gathering place as the worshippers mingled. Bill was introduced to the pastor by Carlos, and he was asked to share something from the pulpit, as we had anticipated. Bill was always up for a challenge, so this did not rattle him a bit.

They must have had English-speaking guests before, because there was a translator among the brethren, and he assured Bill that all would be well. As the worship band began to play, I immediately recognized the song.

"You are Lord. You are Lord. You have risen from the dead, and You are Lord."

Praises can be sung to God in English and in Spanish, and together they become a beautiful melody to His ears. After an extended time of singing, the pastor led us in prayer and then introduced Bill.

I don't remember what he shared, but I do remember how special it was to be there that day. Bill would speak and the translator would do his thing, back and forth. I'm so glad we did not miss this blessing by letting fear or timidity get the upper hand. The people were so warm and friendly, and they hugged us as we left.

Vacations are so needed and wonderfully restful, but nothing beats sharing God's Word and worshipping with His people.

MY OWN PERSONAL MISSIONARY

Teaching kids seemed to be what I was created to do. And that was my training in college and graduate school. I couldn't wait to get my first classroom, which was in 1968, teaching first grade at Ben Franklin Elementary School. I loved going to work each morning and found great satisfaction creating lessons that drew children into the joys of learning. Bill was a planner, and I guess I was also. Our plan was to have me work for about three years to get my permanent certification, then get pregnant with our second child. Billy, our firstborn, was a joy, and we longed to add to our little family. Like clockwork, I gave birth to Beth after teaching three and one-half years, and she was such a blessing to us.

When Beth was about two, I signed up to substitute-teach, and my friend Peggy was able to care for Beth when I worked several days a week. Billy was already in school at this time. As a family, we were doing okay with the schedule until we moved out of town, making my teaching commute longer. My interests also began to change. We had moved into Bethel Covenant Community at this point, and we began to generate ministry such as a ropes course, youth retreats, and marriage weekends. As we adjusted to living "in community" with eight couples at its peak, Bethel was both a blessing and a challenge. I learned to garden, to can multitudinous quarts of tomatoes and green beans, and to share life with my sisters in Christ.

After a handful of years, Bill and I found ourselves becoming more active in our church. I began to yearn to teach adults instead of children. Men's and women's Bible studies, marriage retreats, Sunday school organization, worship, renewal, and evangelism events were a few of the avenues we enjoyed. With raising a family, Bethel obligations, and our church ministries, there was no longer room in my schedule to teach in the local school system. So I stopped.

You have probably wondered about the title of this entry. Bill called me his own personal missionary. At a time in culture where many women my age were in the workforce and contributing to the family income, I quit a paying job and gave volunteer hours on a fairly full-time basis. My husband concurred with and encouraged this family decision. His heart was to serve Jesus as well, but someone had to provide for the bills to be paid, so I got to be the "missionary" for a time. We never regretted that decision.

Looking back on it, I am ever so proud of Bill. The Lord blessed us with his career at IUP and with a very good salary. Sure, the extra money I could have made by teaching would have been nice, but the reward we both experienced doing life this way was God's direction for us. He was proud of me and sensed the calling that God had placed in my heart to serve Him as a volunteer. I felt free to set my own schedule and give the hours I was able, allowing time for family pursuits as well. So much of our ministry was intertwined that freeing me to serve was part of Bill's calling as well as mine.

Bill became my biggest cheerleader in life

THE TRAIN

Bill discovered an interest in model trains when he was a young child. He remembered setting up his train platform in a dirt basement at his home in Lemoyne. My dad bought me a train when I was a child, and Bill incorporated mine and his when we got married. As a new dad, Bill circled Billy's crib with a train track loop so his son would be entertained. One year the trains were set up in my parents' basement and young Billy learned to love trains like his dad.

Trains weren't always prominent in our home. There were many years when they were put away in boxes and stored in the attic. After Bill stopped coaching wrestling in 1985, he began to set up a serious train platform in our Bethel home. The first spot for this new platform was located in the loft above our living room, then it graduated to the garage, taking up the whole room. Lastly, it found a home in our upstairs living room. The setup became so elaborate people would call to check if they could come to see it. We then began to have our "train party," an open house around

Christmastime where we served punch and snacks and friends would come to view the train.

The grandkids loved to see Papa's train. Bill constructed a shelf up high for them to sit on and watch the train. They had seat belts, train hats, and scarves and thought it was all wonderful. It gave them a great vantage point to see all the track, trains, houses, lights, etc.

Bill would take the whole thing down at various times over the years to begin all over again. I couldn't understand that process. Why not just run the train around and enjoy it since it took so much to get it up and going? No, the fun for Bill was in the planning and the strategizing. He loved the challenge of making things different each time and the adventure of it all. But you would have guessed that.

After moving to New Castle, we built a large home with a big game room to hold the train platform. What we didn't count on was that we also had a pool table, ping pong table, player piano, and furniture, so the whole platform had to be downsized.

In retirement, the condo we purchased was just too small for a train platform. We realized that when we bought it, but it seemed a wise purchase, given our age and stage of life. I think that fact made me sadder than it made Bill. I even made suggestions to him of how we could turn the garage into his train room or build something attached to the sunporch. He vetoed those suggestions because he knew they were only of a wife trying to please her husband. He rolled with the punches and had some train track shelves built along the walls in the study so that his special engines and trains could be displayed. Where there is a will, there is a way!

It was a fun and relaxing hobby for Bill, and we've all been the beneficiaries. Billy has an interest in trains and has taken some of them to use in his game room. Grandson Gideon also enjoyed playing train with Papa, and one of the last projects Bill did was to set up a platform for Gideon in his game room. My study still has trains on the walls. I don't plan to ever move them.

SATISFYING DESIRES
AT A LOWER LEVEL

Someone has said, "Sometimes we just satisfy our desires at a lower level." I don't know where we got this quote, but it became something Bill and I would say to each other when we settled for something that brought a bit of comfort and a measure of solace, even if it was a poor substitute for the real thing.

One example of this is clearly etched in my memory. When our son Bill and his wife, Deb, were expecting a new baby, they had the typical scheduled sonogram. I was working in my Graystone Church office when the phone call came telling me there were some serious issues found when the physician read the sonogram. Bill and Deb came over to the office, and together we went to my husband's office at IUP, where he was between classes. We all sat and talked, cried and prayed, and tried to sort out what was being said about this sweet preborn baby who would later be named Joshua David. There were major concerns about many of this child's body parts. They were told that if he made it to full term, the chances of survival were slim. The medical community tried to share the prognosis and the options Bill and Deb had. Abortion was obviously one option.

We are a pro-life family. We believe God is the giver of life, and it is His good gift. We believe that abortion snuffs out life in the womb and is not God's plan. This was now a "rubber meeting the road" issue. Suddenly, this was no longer a sterile concept but a reality. Were we pro-life in theory or in actuality? Bill and Deb had only to think about that for a nanosecond until they were able to confirm what their decision would be. They chose life.

After spending a bit of time together in Bill's office, they left, I left, and Bill taught his last class that day. Later that evening, Bill and I were scheduled to meet with our "dinner for eight" group at the home of one of the couples. I met Bill before we went to the meeting, and we were both pretty shaken. We had about an hour before we were expected at the meeting, so we went to the mall and walked around mostly in silence. Our hearts hurt for our kids. Our "grandparent hearts" hurt as well. We were trusting the Lord with the outcome of this grim report, but what might happen loomed large.

As we strolled, we saw Gardner's, a local candy store that made the best peanut butter melt-aways in the world. We needed comfort and consolation, and at that weak moment we chose to get it from those peanut butter melt-aways. We were satisfying our desires at a lower level. Obviously, sweets were not going to make this situation better, but at that moment we chose them to dull the pain.

When we got to our group meeting, we were able to share our hearts, cry with the group, receive prayer and hugs and God's peace and comfort, the only true solace and consolation.

On occasion, in the years to come, we quoted this saying when we found ourselves choosing the immediate, the easy, the accessible to manage our discomfort as we moved into a place of trust and peace, leaving the situation at the feet of the Father.

WORDS DO MATTER

I have recently become aware of how often I say, "God is good." It is truth. He indeed is good, all the time. The problem for me is not in the truth of the sentence but in the way I have caught myself using it. For instance, I might say, "Today I found that bracelet I had lost. God is good!" The implication in what I said was that God earned His goodness moniker because He helped me find my bracelet. No! No! No! God is good regardless of whether or not I find a bracelet. It might have been better if I had said, "God showed me some of His goodness today by allowing me to find my bracelet."

You might be saying to yourself, "Oh, Linda. What's the big deal here? I know God is good. Let's not be so picky."

I think the big deal, at least for me, is that often our vocabulary subtly reflects our theology. For instance, I might say, "My arthritis in my knees is really bad today. I can hardly come down the stairs." It might be a true-enough statement, but I would rather say, "This arthritis that comes against me is hard today." Subtle? Sure. Important? You bet! Why?

Because I don't like, want, or accept this arthritis. It isn't mine. I don't want it. So why call it mine?

Don't we sometimes say, "Everyone is sick in my family, and I just know I am the next one to get this flu." We indeed may get sick just because germs are real and stuff happens, but I don't need to confess it as fact and talk myself into it.

Scripture says in Proverbs 23:7, "As a man thinks within himself, so he is" (NAS). If we tell ourselves something often enough, it becomes truth in our minds and hearts.

Missionary to the Caribbean, Walford Thompson once said, "What instructs the mind controls the emotions and directs the will." What we think on enough begins to affect how we feel and soon becomes our behavior. If I want to experience truth in my life, then it is important to speak it forth.

This whole topic is not an exercise in nitpicking. What it boils down to is recognizing the words we speak have power and we need to choose them carefully. I am not suggesting that we each become superweird and talk differently than those around us. I'm just sharing that it is so easy to fall into the habit of speaking forth conventional wisdom or lack thereof and not even think what we are saying.

It has become common to ask how someone is doing and to be told, "Not too bad." I am sure that person has heard that response from grandpa and mom and uncle Harry all his life but has never really thought of what he is saying. I don't even really know what that means. Does it mean I am bad but not really all that bad? I so much want to ask the person just how bad he is, but usually I stop before I make a fool out of myself or embarrass the person. Recently, with my sore arthritic knees, I have actually answered a question of how my knees are doing by saying, "Not too bad!" Now that made sense to me.

On Facebook, when someone shares that they need prayer for healing, inevitably there will be a response that says, "Sending good vibes your way" or "Sending my good thoughts to you." One of these days I am going to actually find out how to send "a vibe" across cyberspace. I know how to pray, but send a vibe or a thought, not so much.

Words *do* matter.

NONDELIBERATE TRANSPARENCY

Dr. Timothy Keller is a pastor, preacher, and *New York Times* best-selling author. He was the lead pastor at Redeemer Presbyterian, a large church in New York City. While reading his book *Preaching*, Bill was affected by a concept that Keller called nondeliberate transparency. Keller wrote thus on pages 166–167:

> If you want to preach *to* the heart, you need to preach *from* the heart. It's got to be clear that your own heart has been reached by the truth of the text. This takes non-deliberate transparency. Heart-moving preachers (in contrast to heart-manipulating ones) reveal their own affections without really trying to. What is required is that as you speak it becomes evident in all sorts of ways that you yourself have been humbled, wounded, healed, comforted, and exalted by the truths you are presenting, and that they have genuine power in your life.

Bill Blacksmith wanted to exhibit this character trait. He hoped to share the life lessons that he himself was learning.

Application was very important to him. His desire was not just to disseminate information but to be a vessel by which the Holy Spirit could work transformation in the lives of his class or his congregation. I feel like he achieved that goal. What you saw in him was who he was, imperfect, vulnerable, a sinner saved by grace, and a passionate follower of Jesus Christ.

His commitment to love Jesus was zealous and visible. He occasionally said that the person who most disappointed him was himself. He longed to live a righteous life before his Lord but sometimes failed. Driving his car to the glory of God was one of his greatest challenges. Or maybe his hardest challenge was playing a game with family or friends for fun and not like "cutthroat hopscotch." I remember on several occasions seeing him withdraw from a situation when he sensed he was getting too competitive. I respected him for doing that, but I knew it hurt because he loved to play. His nose-to-the-grindstone attitude had served him well while competing in wrestling and also while fighting for the gospel of Jesus Christ. He was trying to learn when to be intense and when to chill out.

God does not make mistakes in how He creates and calls His children. We are all in the process of working out our salvation with fear and trembling. Life is difficult, but God is eager to fill us with His Spirit and help us to become all that He calls us to be. Scripture tells us that God's Word is living and active, sharper than any double-edged sword. It was written to people long ago and to us as well. As we allow Him to mold us into a vessel that He can use, we, too, can exhibit nondeliberate transparency. What others will see in us is the character of Jesus Christ.

COMIC BOOKS AND EYE DROPS

I had stopped my newspaper for a time because I was away from Indiana. Today I got a Sunday paper at the local convenience store so I could read the Sports page and see my granddaughter's track write-up. She had been doing a great job, and I wanted to be sure to collect all her articles. While riffling through the sections of the Sunday paper to find the Sports page, I saw the comics. Somehow, I was never interested in reading the comics, but Bill was. If I got to the paper first, I always pulled this section out for him to see. It brings a smile to my face now whenever Sunday rolls around and the paper sticks out of the slot beside my mailbox.

Bill did not have happy memories as far as school was concerned. He could name the teachers in his early grades, but the visions that came to mind were bleak, to say the least. I can still hear him tell me about his early elementary years in school and how he learned to read. As an active and probably disinterested boy, he was not enamored by the Dick and Jane books used in those days to teach children. He shared that he learned to read by collecting comic books. He had a huge collection of them and remembered running over to Roger's Store whenever a new shipment of comics came in, then disappearing into his bedroom to read it cover to cover. When he left home for college, his mother cleaned out her attic and threw away all his comic collection, thinking it was just junk. It was probably worth quite a bit of money if sold to a collector. Oh, well!

I'm thinking about this today and how the Lord often uses something mundane and ordinary to accomplish His purposes. Bill, and kids like him, needed to learn to read. Don't we all? And yet the resources available then were mediocre at best. I would not have guessed that comic books would bring the excitement and motivation needed for young minds to engage and stay in the game long enough to develop skills and expertise, but they did in at least this one case. Something so common was used by God to accomplish a good purpose in a young child's life.

Romans 8:28 says, "And we know that God causes all things to work together for good to those who love God, to those who are called according to His purpose" (NAS). I call my eye drops my Romans 8:28 drops. Under my optometrist's orders, I began to use one drop in each eye at bedtime when my eye pressures became dangerously high. High readings can lead to glaucoma, I was told, so the drops help me maintain healthy eyes. And guess what a side effect of the drops is? Long eyelashes! What female doesn't want long eyelashes? A mundane and ordinary thing, but a good outcome for me.

What has the Lord used in your life to help you? Things that start badly may not end that way. God is always at work.

THE ANCIENT OLYMPIC OATH

In July of 2008, in the month before the Summer Olympics in Beijing, Bill preached a three-part series on the ancient Olympic oath, which said, "I will train hard," "I will not quit," and "I will not cheat." The ancient Olympic games, which began in 776 BC, were a very important part of life in biblical times. When the apostle Paul wrote to the various churches in the New Testament, he used the metaphor of the "games" to help explain what it meant to be a fully devoted follower of Jesus Christ.

Bill began his first Olympic sermon by saying, "A few years ago, Linda and I were driving to Ottawa, Canada, to attend the World Congress on Sport Psychology. I was getting tired, and Linda took over the wheel while I took a nap. When I woke up, I realized we were really making good time. Then I saw how fast we were going!

Linda said, "I really like these speed limits in Canada. At one hundred miles per hour, we're zooming right along."

"Sweetheart, in Canada it's kilometers per hour!"

Hearty laughter arose as he concluded that introduction. As you have already guessed, this didn't really happen, but Bill loved to tell stories with me as the subject. He enjoyed telling them so much, and I enjoyed watching the joy on his face when he told them that I played along, and we both knew that no one in the congregation actually believed the story! What a fun-loving man this was that the Lord gave me! He loved to laugh and make people chuckle. His eyes danced as he began one of his stories, and I could always tell one was coming by the way he held his mouth. I often reminded him that he was no good at fibbing because his face forever gave him away.

He continued the sermon on a more serious note.

Research identified what it took to become an Olympic champion. It was the fact that athletes trained hard. On average, it took ten years of deliberate practice to win a gold medal at the Olympics. Working six to eight hours a day, for five or six days a week to develop skill, correct mistakes, and refine expertise, these athletes were a committed group.

Paul says in 1 Corinthians 9:24–25, "Do you not know that in a race all the runners run, but only one gets the prize? Run in such a way as to get the prize. Everyone who competes in the games goes into strict training. They do it to get a crown that will not last; but we do it to get a crown that will last forever" (NIV).

Think of the cost benefit here. Athletes are willing to invest ten years for ten minutes in the world's spotlight, ten minutes of glory. They were willing to pay the price to get a crown, or a medal, that will not last. Paul says that we run the race of life to get a crown that will last forever. Like an athlete, we are called to go into strict training as we grow to be faithful disciples of Jesus Christ.

The second part of the Olympic oath is "I will not quit." Paul writes to Timothy, "I have fought the good fight, I have finished the race, I have kept the faith. Now there is in store for me the crown of righteousness which the Lord, the righteous judge, will award to me on that day— and not only to me, but also to all who have longed for His appearing" (2 Tim. 4:7–8 NIV).

Bill continued to preach. In 1992, the Summer Olympic Games were held in Barcelona, Spain. One of the runners in the four-hundred-meter race was an English athlete named Derek Redmond. He had trained for years to compete in the Olympics, but while sprinting in a qualifying heat, he suddenly pulled his right hamstring and crumpled to the track in pain. Determined to go on, Derek struggled to his feet, fended off medical attendants, and started to hop on one leg to the finish line. Suddenly, a large man in a T-shirt scaled the retaining wall and jumped onto the track. Before anyone could stop him, Jim Redmond reached his son. The young runner leaned on his father's shoulder as he staggered to complete the race. The entire crowd stood and cheered the two men on. When they crossed the finished line, it was as if the runner, his father, and the spectators had done it together. Derek did not quit.

But how disappointing. All Derek had worked for, all those hours of practice, all those years of work, shattered in a moment. Life happens like that sometimes.

The apostle Paul tells us in 2 Corinthians 11 some of the hard things that had happened in his life. He clearly understood persecution, trial, tribulation, and suffering, yet he did not quit.

The third portion of the Olympic oath was "I will not cheat." Bill continued.

In 1932, the gold medal winner of the women's one-hundred-meter dash was found to be a man at his death. In 1988, the gold medal winner in the one-hundred-meter dash was stripped of his medal for using steroids. It was Adolf Hitler who tried to manipulate by using the Olympic Games to promote Nazi Germany and his idea of the superiority of the white race. Nevertheless, who was the hero of the 1936 games in Berlin? Jesse Owens, the young African American from Alabama, won four gold medals.

Cheating is sometimes the world's way of trying to be successful, but never God's way. We are called to the highest standard, the Word of God. What do we teach our children when we tell them to pretend to be younger than they are to get in for a reduced rate at the amusement park? How often have sales clerks given us too much money back or left an item off the bill? How do we handle that? Are we following the rules when reporting our federal income taxes? Or when we illegally copy a CD?

The apostle Paul speaks to this topic in his second letter to Timothy.

> No soldier in active service entangles himself in the affairs of everyday life, so that he may please the one who enlisted him as a soldier. And also, if anyone competes as an athlete, he does not win the prize unless he competes according to the rules. (2 Tim. 2:4–5 NIV)

The sermon applied well to that pre-Olympic time in history, and it applies well to us today. As fully devoted followers of Jesus, we each need to be serious about learning and growing; we need to be tenacious and hang in there even when it seems like we never make progress, and we need to follow God's Word, for it is the Manufacturer's Handbook.

MY GIRL

"Grami, when you hear Papa tell stories about you, doesn't that make you feel uncomfortable?" asked my granddaughter one day when we were discussing Bill's propensity to regale an audience with Linda stories.

"Mostly, no," I replied as I wanted to honestly answer her query. "Your grandfather loves to laugh and make people laugh, and he finds great joy in telling stories about me. Occasionally, when his stories hit a nerve with me, we have a private discussion about it that results in his apology. But usually I'm fine with the stories and I enjoy the laughter. I think the difference between my enjoyment and my embarrassment comes with figuring out his motive. Is he telling this story to simply 'put me down,' or is he just having fun?"

As I thought about her question, I remembered a rule we always taught couples in marriage seminars: "Your compliments you need to make very public, and your complaints keep very private." The idea here was that it was never good to tell tales about your spouse in public with the intention of insulting, maligning, or humiliating them. The kinds of things that should be shared with others would be those character qualities that were appreciated, valued, respected, or prized. Therein lies the explanation of why I could enjoy Linda stories.

One of the ways we can feel most loved is hearing how our spouse talks about us when we aren't present. On many occasions, Bill's colleagues, students, or athletes would share with me an example he used in class or practice about me. It was *always* positive, loving, and complimentary. They would say, "He loves you so much." I knew that when we were not together, he would place me in the best light possible, even when I may not have deserved that position at that time.

Bill often called me "My girl," "My sweet," or "My love." He brought me flowers for no reason, put Post-It Notes on my desk for me to discover, and called me from his office to just tell me he was thinking about me. He also gave me his attention when I needed to talk—well, most of the time. The exception was when a really intense action scene was on TV. I learned to be sensitive to him as well and say that I had something I wanted to talk with him about when it was convenient. He would usually turn off TV when the shoot-'em-up scene was over, and we would talk.

Lest I leave you with the impression that life was always wine and roses in our relationship, it was not. Bill was human, and so am I, so we had many things about which we did not see eye to eye. He used to tell others that we could fight like "cats and dogs." Not sure it was ever that bad, but we did have disagreements. The good thing was that we had learned to "fight fair" and come to a mutual understanding after an argument. We also worked on the scripture from Ephesians 4:26, which said, "In your anger do not sin. Do not let the sun go down while you are still angry, and do not give the devil a foothold" (NIV).

Early on in our relationship, I acquiesced, and things were wonderfully arranged for Bill. Our life was more peaceful, but I never really was able to express my feelings, so he was never sure what I felt or why. After many years, I learned to share and own my feelings, and we both learned to actually hear each other. Communication was big in our marriage, and I am grateful for all the long talks we had as we tried to understand each other. We often said we "talked topics to death," which we sometimes did, but the result was always unraveling the reason for the disagreement. We may not have moved to "agreement," but the goal had been met, respect and understanding.

So did I care if he told and enjoyed Linda stories? Not at all. I knew I was loved and respected.

A ROSE A DAY

My mother outlived my dad by four years. When Dad was living, anytime we all got together, it was with both Mom and Dad. I can't remember spending much time with Mom alone. We just never did mother-daughter things like many of my friends did with their moms. After Dad went to be with Jesus, I decided to plan some trips that Mom and I could do together. I invited her to join me at a woman's retreat at my church. She seemed to like it. We took a road trip to Osceola, where she grew up, and visited several of her friends along the way. One stop was at Mansfield, where she attended college. She really liked that. The best trip was a week in Bradenton, Florida, seeing Mom's sister, my aunt. I was so thrilled that we were able to make the trip since Mom was now in her early eighties.

Three or four days would have been plenty for our Florida trip, but we made reservations for a week before we had thought that out. Our days there consisted of breakfast at home, lunch out at a restaurant, afternoons sitting and remembering days gone by, and dinner at another restaurant. It really was a wonderful time for Mom and my aunt to catch up on old times, but I didn't realize that six days of nonstop talking can get old.

Each morning I would jog to get some exercise and escape a bit to come back to more stories about the good old days. The first day we were there, the doorbell rang with a delivery for me. The package held six long-stemmed red roses with a card that said, "A rose a day until I see you again. Love, Bill." Sometimes his romance meter would hit the top of the chart. My mom and aunt were even impressed.

One day I asked if we could go to the beach. I knew I would enjoy the sunshine, and maybe they would also. Yes. So we packed up and headed for the ocean. What I didn't know was that neither of them wanted to swim or sunbathe, so they sat under a pavilion and watched me as I enjoyed the sun. I read and talked with Bill by phone, all the while under the watchful eye of the sisters who were in the shade.

We ate and talked and walked and ate some more. Soon our time to leave came, and I was ready get home to my husband. As I relive those days in my memory, I realize how precious they were. Mom is now gone, but I am grateful for the times God gave us together. We weren't accustomed to it, but in her later years, we were able to recapture some lost time.

Life is delicate, fragile, and fleeting. When I was younger, my thoughts and actions were often self-absorbed, but as I age, I seem to be gaining a bit of God's wisdom. The people God puts in my life are important to Him and need to be important to me. I forget that when I allow the pressures and stresses to dictate the speed of life.

WATCH THE COMPANY YOU KEEP

Sometimes we shine. We perform extraordinarily well, and we just have to say, "Wow, how did that happen?" God brings forth good things from us, and it surprises us once in a while. It reminds me of the story in Acts 3 and 4 (NIV) about two of Jesus' disciples, Peter and John, who were going to the temple at the time of prayer. They saw a crippled beggar who asked them for money. Peter's response to the man was this: "Silver or gold I do not have, but what I have I give you. In the name of Jesus Christ of Nazareth, walk." God immediately healed the beggar, and he rose to his feet and went "walking and jumping, and praising God." What a fun event. How encouraging! I'm pretty sure Peter and John said, "Wow, how did that happen?"

Peter and John began to talk with the crowd of people who had witnessed this miracle, and the authorities became disturbed because Peter was sharing about Jesus' resurrection. The two disciples were jailed overnight, but the next day, they continued to share the good news of salvation found in Jesus. In Acts 4:13, it speaks of the onlookers when it says, "When they saw the courage of Peter and John and realized that they were unschooled, ordinary men, they were astonished, and they took note that these men had been with Jesus" (NIV).

These men had been with Jesus. They were not seminary professors or pastors. They were not authors, rocket scientists, or members of the "brightest and best club." They were just regular guys who spent time with Jesus. How precious is that?

Because the disciples spent time with Jesus, they had first-hand knowledge of His character and His heart. He taught them, laughed and cried with them, and lived life for three years with them. Because of this close, abiding relationship, the twelve became like their Master. Others marveled at the courage and zeal they saw in Peter and John, and I imagine the other disciples as well.

That description of them can be said of us as well, if we choose. Most of us don't have huge bragging rights on our own, but we do have an ongoing invitation from the King of Kings and the Lord of Lords. He says, "Come unto me" (Matt. 11:28 KJV). The Creator of the universe gives us a personal invitation to hang out with Him. He says, "Abide in me" (John 15:4 ESV). We can respond to this invitation to have a personal relationship with Jesus just as His disciples did. As they grew, so can we. As they became more and more like their Master, so can we.

"Watch the company you keep" is something our parents instructed us as we grew up. They were hoping that we would be discerning about the kind of friends we chose. Our friends could have the propensity to lead us down crooked trails of life.

The converse is also true. If we choose to spend time with Jesus and listen to His direction for us in the Bible, people will know whom we have been around, and life's path will be straighter because of Him.

COME AND HAVE A BETTER SEAT

How fun it is when something happens in life that parallels a Scripture example! I decided to write about this particular one, and I knew the concept of the story, but not where to find it in the Bible. Bill was so good at knowing where scriptural passages were located, but I am slower at finding them. When I don't know the reference, I usually go to my trusty concordance and look up a word in the passage or a word that captures the concept. This time, that trick was not helping. Evidently, I was not looking up the correct words. After asking the Lord to help me find the appropriate passage, I began thumbing through Bill's well-worn, taped-up Bible, the one that Snowy, the California dog, tried to eat. After looking for a while, I found it. Not only did I see the scripture that I had been looking for, but Bill had also placed a Post-It Note three-fourths of the way down the page with the details of the story I was remembering. Thank you, sweetheart.

The scripture teaches about seeking honor, and it tells about how Jesus addressed this issue in Luke 14:7–11. He saw that people would often rush to grab the seats of honor at a function, so He said it was better to take a lesser seat than a better one. The practical reason for that was, if someone more important came, you might get bumped out of your excellent seat and then you would be humiliated. A more prudent course of action was to take a lesser seat and allow for the host to notice you are way at the back and honor you by calling you to sit up at a better place.

Having read this passage before, I found it was fun to have it played out in our life. We were invited to a wedding celebration by new friends. We hit it off immediately with this couple and were happy to attend their ceremony and reception. Our dilemma was that we were so new to the relationship that we felt a bit uncomfortable. We really had not expected to be invited in the first place. So when we entered the reception hall, we gravitated to the back and found two places at a table in the corner.

This placement was really fine with us, but after a short time, the groom saw us and called us up to the front and placed us at a table with his parents. Oh my! How did that happen? We weren't trying to be humble in our choice of tables. It just seemed like a logical place to be. Sometimes God just wants to surprise us with an unexpected blessing.

> When someone invites you to a wedding feast, do not take the place of honor, for a person more distinguished than you may have been invited. If so, the host who invited both of you will come and say to you, 'Give this man your seat'. Then, humiliated, you will have to take the least important place. But when you are invited, take the lowest place, so that when your host comes, he will say to you, 'Friend, move up to a better place'. Then you will be honored in the presence of all your fellow guests. For everyone who exalts himself will be humbled, and he who humbles himself will be exalted. (Luke 14:7–11 NIV)

WHAT DOES GOD PRIZE?

In my ladies' life group one morning, I asked them if they ever had a "sinful heart." Several seemed shocked with the question, while others promptly nodded to the affirmative. I confessed that I have had to face the fact that I sometimes harbor an "unclean heart." God can see my sin as He looks within.

My mind went immediately to a Bible example of how God deals with sin. When Israel's first king, Saul, failed because of his pride and disobedience to God, the prophet Samuel tells us that God chose another to be king, one with a heart that pleased Him. The one God chose was a shepherd boy named David. We know from reading this passage in 2 Samuel 11:1–12:13 that David was very imperfect. This story is tragic in many ways. David's actions displeased God, and there were severe consequences. Yet we are told that David was a man after God's own heart. How can this be? What made David acceptable to the Lord with sin in his life?

In 1 Samuel 16:7, it says that we as humans often look at outward appearances, but God looks beyond the surface and looks into our hearts. What did God see in David's heart that tipped the balance? I think it was the way David handled his sin. He was not faultless; he was guilty. He was not sinless; he was full of sin. David did not hide his sin but chose to openly confess his sin humbly before his God. He did not rationalize it like Saul but repented. "I have sinned," he declared (2 Sam. 12:13 NIV).

In Psalm 51, David confesses his sin and asks for forgiveness. David is open, authentic, and candid before his Lord. He had a heart, a passion, a preference for God alone, and when he failed, he repented. When we repent, we do a 180-degree change of direction. We stop going one way and turn around and take the opposite road.

God shows His love in many forms, but one method we may not always identify as love is His correction. I enjoy talking out loud with God. It helps me keep my mind focused and helps deter mental woolgathering. In my talks with Him, I am also trying to listen. He is faithful to show me where I am not seeking after His heart, where I have missed the mark of His perfect plan for me, or where my sin has caused others heartache or distress. That is real love. He accepts me as I am but does not plan to let me stay there without His correction.

God's Word tells me that when I confess my sin, He is faithful and will forgive me. Like David, if I am open, authentic, and candid before Him, He enables me to change direction and go a new way. He also calls me to make situations right when I have hurt others.

One morning the leadership team of Alpha had joined hands to pray together. As we each voiced our petitions to our Father, one of the men thanked God for the good work he perceived I had done getting the lesson ready. Another pitched in to agree with that thanksgiving. As I stood with head bowed and eyes closed, I began to feel God's conviction. I had not been the one that put hard work into that lesson, but I was being praised for it. A small thing? Perhaps. But I couldn't shake the uncomfortable feeling. After we said Amen, I had a choice.

At first, I reasoned it was far easier to let it go and remain silent. No one really cared, and besides, we were supposed to start class soon. But God cared. If I confessed that it was not me, I would be embarrassed. It should have been me, but someone else stepped in to help, and I was getting the credit. Before we left the circle, I reluctantly told the group that the praise should go to someone else. I was not the one who prepared the lesson. God had allowed me to make a course correction in a very small thing. Although minor, learning to respond to God's prompting in the little things of life prepares us to be obedient in larger ways. I am not always obedient. I don't always heed the conviction of the Spirit. It is so easy to rationalize and slough it off. It is far less embarrassing to let it go and move on. But is that what God prizes?

When God makes me aware of my unclean heart, I'm able to go to the Lord and ask for His forgiveness. I'm able to go to the one I have offended and ask for their forgiveness also. By His working in my life and His forgiveness, my heart is washed clean. That is a great gift of love that He gives to His obedient children. We can all be people after God's own heart. His ways are right and perfect, and He wants us to live according to His direction. The question for me and for each of us is this: Is it our desire to please Him in all of life or to go our own way, ignoring or rejecting His direction? We have a choice.

TOGETHER WE ARE 130 YEARS OLD

I like going to the movie theater. It is one of my favorite date venues. I know, I can watch movies on DVDs or when they come out on Netflix or Amazon Prime cheaper, but I love the experience of actually sitting in the theater and seeing a film on the big screen. The popcorn is a bonus.

I want to tell you about a date we had when we were each sixty-five years old, and by telling it I am making myself and my sweet husband very vulnerable. We often had it together and were fairly rational, but not this night. As you read this tale, you may not find it amusing, but as I sit at my computer, it brings forth belly laughs. Since I am the writer, I can choose the material.

It began by me sharing with Bill about a movie I hoped to see. I watched the paper and was thrilled when it came to town. I even cut out the newspaper clipping to remind me I wanted to see it.

Bill was not the theater fan I was. He would rather sprawl out on the recliner and enjoyed the movie in his sweats, where he could pause the action and make a refrigerator run, or two, or three. Nevertheless, he knew I loved to go out, so when he heard me say that this special movie was coming, he invited me to go on a date to the theater.

The night came that we had decided to go, and I got ready and was glad to hop in the car and be on our way. As we entered the theater, I took the lead and went up to the young gal that was selling tickets. I had actually forgotten the name of the movie, so I was scanning the marquis above her head as she patiently waited, and I mumbled that we needed two senior tickets. I was a little embarrassed that I just couldn't remember the name of the movie. Bill had never learned the name of the movie in the first place. He was just taking me, and that was all he needed to know.

After Bill heard me say that we were seniors, he chimed in with a grin, "Together we are 130 years old."

He often liked to be funny (or tried to be), especially when speaking to a younger person. He had a great sense of humor, but sometimes I failed to find the humor in what he said. I'm sure the teenager thought she was dealing with two dementia patients who had just escaped from the local hospital.

By this time, I had remembered the name of the movie but could not see it written on the marquis. I told the girl the movie's name, and she said it was no longer playing.

"Oh, yes, it is!" I replied. "See, it is written right here," I said as I pulled out the newspaper clipping from my pocket and proudly showed her.

"That was last week's paper," the exasperated ticket seller responded.

I think we just picked another movie quickly or sheepishly stepped aside to let the others in line get their tickets. This is all so funny to me now as I reflect. It is amusing on so many levels. Thinking about it now warms my heart and tickles my old funny bone.

Laughter is so good for us. Life can often be too serious, and it is important to enjoy the journey.

WE AREN'T CHEAP, WE'RE THRIFTY

We found a wine we liked while vacationing in Cape May, New Jersey, one year. It was from Argentina and was extremely inexpensive. I am not sure what it did to our intestinal tract as we drank it, but it tasted good. Bill and I weren't big drinkers but did enjoy wine on occasion. When we left the beach, we bought a case of our special pick to take home. After paying the bill, we did the math, and each individual bottle cost us only $1.50. What a bargain! I was proud of our thrifty purchase and had visions of enjoying this wine far into the future.

Later that year, we received an invitation to a dinner party from a new acquaintance and her husband. We always tried to take an appropriate hostess gift when visiting someone, so voilà, why not take a bottle of our new wine?"

Is that too cheap a gift to take?" I asked myself. "No one will know. It is an obscure brand. We like it, and so will they. Why not?"

Fast-forward to the night of the party. Their home was lovely and decorated impeccably. Other couples were also invited, and when we knocked at the huge front door, I felt a bit out of place. A large chandelier graced the stairway, and lush Oriental rugs softened our step as we entered. The host graciously received our gift and ushered us into the living room. There was lively conversation as we were treated to crystal wineglasses filled with white or red, our choice, and dainty appetizers. It was all very exquisite.

Before dinner, Mr. Host brought a bottle of red wine around and told us the story of how he came to discover it. Apparently, this wine was very expensive, $150 a bottle, and he had found it on one of his international business trips. He was so proud to pour us a small glass, and it was good, but I had never in all my days tasted wine that expensive. How slow should I drink it? I needed to make this last. The friends seated around the table sipped and lauded this special drink as the meal was served.

After a delicious dinner and great evening, we excused ourselves to leave. The host walked us to the door and handed us a bottle of the "gold-plated, diamond-studded wine." He said he wanted us to have it. We were a bit appalled. We had given Mr. and Mrs. Host a $1.50 bottle of wine, and they gave us wine worth $150. We felt extremely cheap as we walked to our car but found ourselves giggling all the way home.

"Surely hope they never discover the cost of our wine," we said, snickering. "We won't ever be asked back there!"

Since it really was so expensive, we decided to save it for our fiftieth anniversary, which was twelve years hence. We put it in our cold storage in the basement and forgot about it. Several moves later, we decided to keep the bottle in the kitchen pantry so we could pull it out for that special celebration, which, by that time, was right around the corner.

On June 28, 2013, our family gathered in celebration of our fifty years together. It was very special for all of us to be there, and we told the story of the cheap and expensive wine exchanges and broke out the long-anticipated bottle. Small plastic cups were used as we poured the red liquid and raised them up for a toast.

Never was there such disappointment as all faces grimaced and spit out the drink into their napkin or on the kitchen island. That beautiful bottle had gone bad because we did not know how to properly store it, I guess. No one could even take a second sip. It was awful.

The moral to this story is, it really doesn't pay to save things for special occasions. Every day is special. God gives us the gift of life, each day created just for us. Use it now. Do it now. Enjoy it in the present. So often I have heard people say that they will travel when they retire or use that tablecloth just for Christmas. Why not now?

NIGHT-BLOOMING CEREUS

Bill's parents had a large plant that they kept on their enclosed sunporch. At some point near the start of our fifty-four-year marriage, we inherited the plant. In and of itself, it really was a gangly, misshapen eyesore, but when flowers from it bloomed, it was magical. This plant is part of the cactus family, and whenever it chose to do so, it would sprout a tiny bud that grew over a couple of weeks into a full, tight flower ready to burst. And burst it did! The only problem was that it bloomed only at night and just for one night. The flower opened up about 10:00 p.m., and by 8:00 a.m. it wilted. So you can see that in order to enjoy it, you had to be prepared to stay up late or set your alarm to capture it at just the right moment. The blossom was white, extremely fragrant, and four or five inches across, so it was a magnificent sight. More than one blossom might grow on any plant. We never knew what to expect. After many years, we discovered that placing those fertilizer spikes around the base of the plant promoted more flowers.

Life was busy, so we watered it and paid attention when it bloomed, but I have to say the plant survived in spite of us. Bill repotted it when it got too root-bound, but it sat in our living room without much fanfare most of the time. When we moved in to our condo, which was our last home, we knew that two very large plants would not work, so we parted with one of them. The remainder plant found its home on the back patio after the frost subsided in spring and before the weather got too cold in the fall. This plant loved its new home. It grew larger than ever and was difficult to get through the man door to the garage when we brought it indoors for the winter.

If I maneuvered correctly, I was able to get the plant onto a dolly that Bill had made, and I could move it in and out of the garage by myself. Without Bill, I needed to figure out how to do that. My sons, friends, and neighbors would be pleased to help me, but I really wanted to do things myself if I could. For the last two years, the night-blooming cereus has bloomed extraordinarily well. The first summer, it had eighteen blossoms, and last summer it had twenty-two. I alerted my neighbors when I thought the blooms were due to burst because I didn't want to enjoy them all by myself. But having a plant party between the hours of ten and eight might be frowned upon in a mostly retired person neighborhood.

Now, I am in the "baby plant" business. I researched how to trim the mother plant and repot the clippings. I have had two "litters" of babies, and when I tell others that the mother plant is over fifty years old, everyone seems to want one. This past fall I really gave "Mama" a rather-severe haircut. She had grown too big to get through the door, and I was not about to schlep the dolly and humongous plant all around the yard to enter by the regular garage door.

I am waiting to see if she recoups from her haircut.

WHERE IS HE?

I hear stories about widows going to visit their husbands in the cemetery. I get that. The pain of separation is unbearable sometimes, and just being physically close to him is what you need. That concept, even though somber and sad, has brought a smile to my face from time to time.

I need to start by saying that it is good for couples to talk at length about end-of-life issues. Bill and I had decided to be cremated when the time came. The Bible does not really say anything that would prohibit that, and it seemed the best ecological choice to make. We reasoned that when Jesus comes back and the dead in Christ rise and get new bodies, it wouldn't matter if our old bodies had decayed in the ground or been eaten by fish in the sea or had undergone cremation. So that decision was made together long before I was faced with making it alone.

After Bill was cremated—no, let me rephrase that. Bill was not cremated. Bill's spirit, that part of Bill that was his personality and his being, went to be with Jesus. What was left was his body. So let me start again. After Bill's body, his earthly home, was cremated, I needed to do something with the ashes. We had decided that our ashes would be mixed together and then buried after we both died. That necessitated an urn or box or something in the meantime.

I reasoned that maybe I could find a box of some sort on Amazon that would suffice at a lower cost than at the funeral home. I ordered one, and it came in the mail. I rejected it immediately. No, it had to be something nicer than that splintery, ugly box. The funeral director had given me a catalog with lots of choices of urns, boxes, whatever. But this one needed to be large enough for two sets of ashes. Guess what? They actually have double urns, so I guess we were not the first couple to devise this scheme. I spent more than I wanted, but now, on a shelf in our study sits a lovely round wooden receptacle looking a bit like a hatbox containing Bill's ashes, with room for mine.

I didn't choose to display an urn in my living room. I rarely think about it being on the bottom shelf in the study or what is in it. It's just part of the décor of that room at this point. Going back to the beginning of this story, there are days when I want to be close to Bill and go to the cemetery where we have a headstone. But wait, his ashes are not there. They are in the study. But wait, he is neither in the cemetery nor in the study. He is with Jesus in heaven.

Jesus said in John 14:1–3, "Do not let your hearts be troubled. Trust in God; trust also in me. In my Father's house are many rooms; if it were not so, I would have told you. I am going there to prepare a place for you. And if I go and prepare a place for you, I will come back and take you to be with me that you also may be where I am" (NIV).

This confusion of where he is has actually made me smile. Think about it. I don't have to travel to the cemetery to feel close to him. I don't even have to walk from the living room into the study to do it. I just have to talk with Jesus in prayer, and it causes me to feel closer to Bill. I don't pretend to know all that happens when we die. A lot of it is a mystery to me. I just know that I can lean on His promises and trust that one day, like Bill, I will also be with Jesus.

THE A-TEAM

Bill was so skilled at ministering to those who were sick. I think that was largely because he, himself, knew what it was like to be in the hospital during the whole kidney transplant saga.

Scripture says in 2 Corinthians 1:3, "Praise be to the God and Father of our Lord Jesus Christ, the Father of compassion and the God of all comfort, who comforts us in all our troubles, so that we can comfort those in any trouble with the comfort we ourselves have received from God" (NIV).

Bill's heart was compassionate, and he learned by experience how it feels to be helpless, powerless, and dependent on others. He experienced how others ministered to him. Besides being hospitalized during the actual transplant, Bill had a series of stubborn urinary tract infections that landed him in a hospital bed more than once. People would visit, call, and send cards, all promising to pray for him. How wonderful it is to be part of the body of Christ, God's family of believers, and receive the love and care of Christians!

One special friend, Jack, not only promised to pray during one hospital stay but also said, "Bill, let's pray right now," as he began to lift the situation to Jesus over the phone. That ministered to Bill's heart and was a valuable lesson to the both of us. It was an example of ministry to others and began our realization that praying "right now" for people is often the right thing to do. We learned to do that at the grocery store, at church, at the post office, or wherever the conversation pointed to a need. We realized that we needed to use discernment to make sure it was wanted by the person on the other end, but it was a valuable ministry tool that people appreciated.

We soon realized that God was calling us to partner with folks in the hospital or those going through a trauma or family crisis so that we could help bring them support and care. We were empty nesters for the most part and could juggle our schedules to be able to go where needed. Praying with people in crisis has been a privilege God gave us, and Bill was so good at it.

Recently, I was able to visit a special friend in the hospital and ran into one of our forever friends from church, Kevin. Kevin was one of Bill's favorite people, and when I entered the hospital room, Kevin was just leaving. He told me later that he felt good about me arriving and felt like "now the A-Team is here." Wow! What a humbling statement. If anyone was the A-Team, it was Bill. I saw myself as his support, and I was along to learn and to help. For Kevin to refer to me alone as the A-Team took me aback. I am certainly not in the "A" category.

After mulling that day over in my mind, I realize that all of us are on the A-Team as we minister in Jesus' name. When we bring the love of God into any difficult situation, we are operating with His power and His direction. People in crisis need to know that God loves them and that He is there with them. We all can choose to be vessels of hope and encouragement to others. When we show up, when we offer love and help, and when we pray, we are surely a part of God's A-Team.

A LESSER LIFE

It was January 1, 2019, and the beginning of a new year. I sat on my sunporch with my Bible in my lap and my journal on my TV tray, which serves as a desk when I sit there during my quiet time. It was cold outside but cozy for me thanks to the gas heater Bill installed. I was thanking God for the life He gave me, and I wrote these words, "I am grateful for my life, even though it is a 'lesser life' than I had before." A lesser life? Really?

I was reading in Romans that day, and I stopped to ponder Romans 15:13, "May the God of hope fill you with all joy and peace as you trust in Him, so that you may overflow with hope by the power of the Holy Spirit" (NIV).

The words *hope, joy, peace,* and *trust* jumped out at me. I had hope and peace, most of the time, but wasn't feeling much joy at the moment. I had to remind myself of what I know. I seem to be doing a lot of that lately. When emotions latch on to negative circumstances, I need to remind my heart of what is truth.

I know that *joy* is a word very different from the word *happiness*, but they are sometimes used interchangeably. Happiness comes from pleasure-producing circumstances and is dependent on those circumstances. When things are going well, I can be happy. When the bottom drops out, I move from happy to sad or anxious. Joy, on the other hand, is that "deep-down giggle," that feeling of peace and contentment that has nothing whatsoever to do with what is going on in life. Joy, for me, is what I feel when I can sit back and know that all is well because I'm a child of God, and He has my life under His control.

I'm not feeling happiness right now. My circumstances shout to me that I have "a lesser life" than a couple of years ago. But to be honest, I am stronger in feeling joy than ever before. As I sit in the presence of Jesus, I feel His love and protection, and I sense His care for me. He has provided a multitude of friends and a caring and attentive family for me, and I am not alone. This single life does not have to be a lesser one. Yes, it is certainly different, and it is not always welcomed emotionally. God's broad shoulders can withstand my ingratitude and my whining during my pity parties, but He has shown me that He does not intend to let me alone to wallow in my tears.

He has adopted me into His forever family. One day I will cross the finish line and be in His presence forever. When I contemplate this broken, sinful, and unholy world we live in, I want to hasten that day. Lord, help me to overflow with Your Spirit so others see Jesus in me. Help me to run this race to Your honor and glory. And may I do it with joy.

WALKING A NEW PATH

My neighbor Elaine mentioned that she liked to walk and asked me if I wanted to join her. It was a lovely invitation, and I did like to walk, but Bill and I walk together. At least we did. I had only so many steps in my knee arsenal before I got too sore and stiff to go on, and all my steps were with Bill. Most of everything was with Bill. By choice, we did spend most of our leisure time together. Now he was gone.

As long as I can remember, time with my girlfriends was not primary in my life. Oh, I enjoyed sleepovers where we giggled way into the night, cheerleading practice on the school parking lot in the August heat, and pizza parties after football games, but I always seemed to have a boyfriend that took away from girlfriend time. Then Bill came along, and I spent as much time as I could with him. Since we were married right after my senior year in high school, my college experience was not typical. He was my best friend and my life partner. I had been with him since I was sixteen. All of a sudden, things were different.

In our years of ministry, I attended and usually led a ladies' Bible study. It was a joy for me to share truths that were found in God's Word with other women, and I enjoyed their company, but seldom did I spend a Friday evening with a group of women. Friday was date night for Bill and me. I never took a trip with girlfriends. I preferred Bill's company. When we went to the gym, it was the two of us. Now I was a widow. Oh, how I hated that label.

I told Elaine that day I would like to walk with her sometime, but after she left my driveway, I went in the house and cried. It was not that I wanted to cloister myself at home with no one to talk to or laugh with or share the ups and downs of life with; I just didn't know how. My relationship with Bill was comfortable and easy and relaxed. We could talk or not. There was no script or plan to be followed. I could just be me. I knew the time had come for me to learn to do life in a new way. I wasn't sure I even wanted to.

"Lord, I need You to change my heart. I want to enjoy being with my female friends. They aren't Bill and never will be Bill, but You can do a work in my life in this new season and give me companions as I run this race. I am scared, and I need Your help."

In some ways, I had to pick myself up by the scruff of my neck and make myself try some new things. I decided not to wait for others to invite me places; I could initiate outings. I might sit in a new pew at church. I could even have a dinner party like we used to have. People still enjoy being invited out for a meal, right? Why not start a ladies' life group in my home? Maybe invite some widows?

Changes don't come easy, and I still struggle from time to time, but God has been melting and molding me as the weeks and months pass. I am grateful for the new friends I have made and the acquaintances who are becoming like family to me. And my family members who are cherished friends.

"Thank You, Lord. You have taken my wounded heart, opened it, and filled it with new relationships. I am grateful."

It's a beautiful day. I think I will text Elaine and see if she wants to walk.

BLESSED TO BE A BLESSING

God gives us material blessings for our own enjoyment, and sometimes for others to enjoy as well. Our home in Murrells Inlet is one such blessing. We looked for somewhere the family could go for vacation or respite. We found it in 2013. Our little Southern home is located in a gated community only an eight-minute drive from the ocean, and just south of Myrtle Beach. It is removed enough from all the hype of vacationers and yet near enough to activities, restaurants, and most importantly, the airport. By using Spirit Airlines, we can park our car without cost and fly in just over an hour from north to south. As we contemplated retirement, we could see ourselves with our toes in the sand and our time spent traveling between Murrells Inlet and Indiana, Pennsylvania.

An important concept to remember is this: "There is no retirement in the kingdom of God." That was a driving force for us in those early years of retirement. We found some ministry opportunities in both north and south churches, but an unfulfilled longing still existed. "Lord, how do you want to use us in this season of life?"

Together we loved Southern living. Pawleys Island Community Church was wonderful. We got involved in a fellowship group that met for a meal and study each week, and Bill was occasionally asked to teach that group. Our Southern church pastor Don and Ginny and our new friends were awesome, and we fit right in when we were there. During a couple of the years after our purchase, we split our time equally between north and south. It was the best of both worlds.

In the North we were close to our family and were able to follow their activities. Bill volunteered to help the high school wrestling team and thus spend time with grandson Caleb and, after a few years, with grandson Gideon. He so enjoyed teaching them ways to be successful on the mat. Seeing Josh and Luke in their classrooms at the Children's Institute Day School was a treat. Both of these boys had special needs, and this school was a great blessing for their family. During track-and-field season, we saw Michaela run and jump and could visit grandson Matt as he attended the University of Pittsburgh. Matt and Rachel were planning to be married sometime after graduation, and Bill anticipated that he would officiate at their wedding. Being in the North also meant we could travel a bit to visit our foster son, Rick, and his wife, Brenda, and see our granddaughter Desire and her husband, Travis, and children, Tabitha and Maverick. They lived two hours away, but we saw them when we could. Bill had the privilege of marrying Desire and Travis, which warmed our hearts. Lots of good things.

We used our Southern home to bless our family and others. It was comfortable, easy, and fun to offer friends a few days of leisure at the beach. We were blessed to be a blessing to others, and we tried to use our home that way. Obviously, we also used it for our own relaxation.

The house has lost some of its charm without Bill's presence. His old college surfboard hangs on the wall of the TV room alongside his rock climbing ropes and pitons. I see our bench out back with the sign "Grow Old with Me, the Best Is Yet to Be" beside it and his desk with Post-It Note stuck here and there. The cement patio that he designed stretches along the back, and I can still see him collecting the errant golf balls that made their way into our backyard from the golf course. As long as I own this home, I will try to see it as a blessing that I can share with others. It may not be as much fun for any of us now that Bill is not here, but I plan to keep it until we no longer enjoy what it has to offer.

BEACH WALKS AND SHELL TREES

There was a stretch of sand from the north beach of Huntington Beach State Park toward the jetty that was far in the distance. We loved to walk hand in hand along this ribbon of sand and end up at the jetty, which we estimated was about four miles round trip. Before my knees became an issue, we walked it often while visiting our home in Murrells Inlet. My Fitbit told me when we walked that particular beach jaunt, I could be assured of ten thousand steps.

We would collect shells as we walked and put them in our pockets to take home to the shell jar sitting on the end table, where we dated them and dropped them in. Along our path was a curious clump of driftwood that we called the shell tree. Every time we strolled this way, we saw seashells hanging from the branches. I found it strange that there were always shells on the tree even after gusting winds and heavy rain. Why was that? We reasoned that it must be a thing on this beach that those who passed by would automatically pick up shells and decorate the tree, a sort of unwritten rule that no one told us about. We joined the party and did the same each time we were there.

On one particular beach stroll, I said to Bill, "Someday one of us will be doing this alone. I'm not sure I could handle doing this without you." All of a sudden, I find myself doing just that.

We often talked about how good God was to give us a long stretch of years together. At our age, we knew that one day one of us would die. I now am very glad we talked about this. We talked about everything. There is very little that I have questions about now that I am alone, since I felt we had discussed everything. Actually, there is one thing. On Bill's desk blotter, he used to jot down thoughts, prayers, ideas, things he felt God was saying to him. There is that one notation, cryptic, unknown. I can't read it. Was it something he wanted to do or see or say? Wish he were here for me to ask.

On my first visit back to the beach without Bill, I decided to walk that path alone because it held so many wonderful memories. Why not remember? The alternative to facing the pain of special places is to deny myself the very thing that made that place special. I decided I was going to continue to experience the things Bill and I enjoyed. That particular day was beautiful, with bright sunshine and tremendous puffy clouds silhouetted against the blue sky. Singing, sharing my heart with Jesus, and talking to Bill through tears were the agenda of the day. He wasn't physically there with me, but he was ever so much with me in my heart and mind. We were again walking together.

I'D LOVE TO HAVE A PELICAN

Walking along the beach, we would always see pelicans. They would fly in groups above our head as we sloshed in the surf, kicking up sand and foam. How fun and unusual it was to see them dive from high in the air down into the water to catch fish. I wonder how they can see the fish from up so high. I guess they just have great eyesight. What an unusual bird God created!

As we sat on the deck of our favorite restaurant on the marsh walk, munching our shrimp and crab fondue appetizer and sipping our Merlot, I spotted a huge pelican sitting on top of a pylon along the dock. He sat quietly for several minutes, allowing me time to aim and shoot his picture. I loved pelicans. The picture turned out so well that I had it enlarged and framed it. That picture now sits on my dresser in Indiana.

Bill knew I liked pelicans, so when we browsed the shops of Pawleys Island or Murrells Inlet, we were on the lookout for a small pelican replica that I could get to remind me of those special birds. It wasn't hard to find them. We saw some that were made of metal, some plastic, and others captured in shiny jewelry. I never quite saw one that called my name, though. They were nice, but not what I was looking for. After a time, I forgot that I had expressed the desire to have my own pelican.

Guests were visiting one spring, and we were showing them the sights of our lovely getaway home. One of our go-to places was a cute little shopping center that contained interesting boutique stores. Of course, the women had to visit the clothing stores and the guys browsed to find something more to their liking. Finishing up our shopping in the first store, my friend and I were headed next door. As I walked outside, I saw Bill trotting along like a "man on a mission." He was carrying a large package wrapped in brown paper. It looked ever so much like the stump of a tree. "Why in the world did Bill buy a wood stump? Maybe it is a stool for outside around the firepit?"

He didn't see me watching him zoom to the car, and I continued my shopping and forgot about the stump. A couple of days later was my birthday. He walked me into the TV room to show me my gift, which he had carefully moved from the trunk of the car to the house. There on the bookshelf stood the biggest, most elaborate carved wooden pelican that I had ever seen. It was every bit of three feet tall and sat on a base that looked like a tree stump.

I would always tease Bill that his motto was "Bigger is better." He would deny it, but it was so very true. This huge pelican was the coolest gift and no ordinary trinket. All I wanted was a small replica of a pelican, but what I got was such a reminder of my husband's extravagant love and bigger-than-life personality.

OUR STUDY

As I look out the window from my computer chair, I can feel the chill in my bones. The temperature has dropped, and it just started to rain, which adds to the raw feeling of the day. The study in my northern condo is warm and inviting, so all is well. This room was probably originally meant to be a downstairs bedroom, but with our two big rolltop desks, two large chairs, our computer and bookshelves, we needed to make it a place to work. The upper walls near the ceiling are lined with trains placed on metal shelves. Below the trains are our diplomas from Fuller Theological Seminary, letters in beautiful frames that Billy wrote to affirm both of us, my dad's painting of the mountain lion and grandson Caleb's, letter written about Bill during high school where Caleb called him his "personal hero."

This room is probably the most disheveled of any of my rooms, especially right now. I placed another long narrow table in there to hold my papers as I write this book. There are not very many horizontal surfaces clear. I still have Bill's desk and chair, and it will probably stay where it is for a long time to come. He had his quiet time each day at that desk, and his Bible is still open to 2 Samuel where he was reading. I have moved a few things to dust but don't want to change it just yet.

My rolltop desk is where I do my bookkeeping for my household. The writing surface is full of things that need my attention, but the top is full of reminders of Bill. I have framed the picture of us kissing along the rocks of a pond in Maine, where we vacationed in 2010. There is a professional picture of him in a gray sport coat that I loved. I think I kept it in the closet upstairs because I did not want to let it go. There is also the picture of us outside by the Bracken family pool. It is one of my favorites. Facing me by the computer is our picture taken at Grace Chapel during our ministry there. Family shots are everywhere. A picture of Caleb wearing his Navy uniform sits near the desk lamp. A collage of Bill baptizing Beth and Ed in their pond holds special memories. The four-generation picture of my mom (whom the kids called Bam), Beth, Michaela, and me.

I love the picture of the three Blacksmith boys Josh, Matt, and Luke. Josh went to heaven six weeks before Bill. He was twenty-two years old. Luke will soon be eighteen. Josh and Luke had the same health challenges, which made life interesting for their family. Matt is now working toward his doctorate in human genetics at the University of Michigan.

The bookshelves are full of commentaries, Bibles, study books, and resources we have used over our years in ministry. We had to give away many books when we moved from New Castle. Why are books so hard to discard? Bill came up with a creative, although mischievous, way to do this by stuffing smaller books into the cushions of a friend's couch before we left life group one evening. I'm sure that was appreciated. Not!

A white fabric box is on the bottom shelf of the bookcase to the right of the round wooden urn containing Bill's ashes and, at some future date, to hold mine. The white box carries all the cards, letters, emails, etc. that I received after Bill went to heaven. People are so kind.

How can one room hold so many memories? I find it a peaceful place to work as I remember. I am grateful God has given me this room, this home. He is Jehovah-Jireh, my provider.

THE FOSBURY FLOP

One of Bill's greatest gifts from the Lord was the gift of encouragement. It was manifested in various ways as he lived his life. He was forever teaching something to someone. I have a special gift from Beth on my desk. It is a shadowbox containing pictures of Bill with each of the Bracken children. The pictures show him in various situations where each child was listening intently to what he was telling them.

One way Bill taught about life was to share stories. One such story was prompted after watching Michaela high-jump in one of her track meets. Bill told me about high jumper Dick Fosbury, gold medalist in the 1968 Olympics, who first introduced the Fosbury flop. He had taught about this sport hero in his psychology of sport classes.

"People thought, how strange—to jump over the high bar backward! But now we know that world records are being set by this one-time anomaly. High jumpers have used this method with great success," he said.

Bill continued to make a life application from the story. "Sometimes we have to do things differently to raise the bar, to become better." As I listened, I began to ponder how that principle applied to my own life. My own walk of faith? Where do I need a Fosbury? What do I need to do differently?

Life lessons often take a while to settle in and become reality. Recently, I was able to do a Fosbury in my daily schedule. It was right after Bill went to heaven that I began to conceive this book in my heart. Maybe all good things have to begin with a lot of thought, prayer, and minimum action, I don't know, but that is how I began. I talked with the Lord about it and set up a system of filing entries. Little by little I created text while sitting at my computer desk. It was fun and ever so healing to reflect and share my memories and thoughts. Over time I collected quite a few entries or chapters.

When people would ask me what I was doing with my time in this new season of life, I was quick to respond that I was "writing a book." It felt good to have a project and to be purposeful in this pursuit. During the winter of 2020, I realized that in order to actually complete this book, I needed to have a goal and be diligently working on it. It wasn't good enough to announce to others that I was doing it. I had to actually be accomplishing something. So I decided to take a hiatus from several of my commitments and work on writing for at least ten hours per week. That may not seem like a lot of time for seasoned authors, but for me it was a great challenge. As I type this entry, I am completing week 5 of trying to create something book-worthy for ten hours each week. I have seen the book "take off" in my mind and in reality.

I am grateful for this Fosbury in my life. I am more eager now to discover other changes that the Lord will bring in His time.

GROW OLD WITH ME

> For when David had served God's purpose in his own
> generation, he fell asleep.

> —Acts 13:36 NIV

This scripture was one that Bill referred to often. As I think about it now, it brings me comfort. To me, it says that God has a plan, and when David had fulfilled God's plan for his life, God called him home. What a beautiful picture of God's sovereignty.

Ecclesiastes 3 says, "There is a time for everything and a season for every activity under heaven: a time to be born and a time to die" (NIV).

Psalm 90:10 says, "The length of our days is seventy years—or eighty, if we have the strength" (NIV). This Psalm reminds each of us of the brevity of life and our eternal home. Each day is a gift, and we should make each day count.

I watched Bill transition from this life to the next on that Wednesday afternoon about 3:17. I had the strong feeling that this verse written about David was true for Bill Blacksmith as well. When Bill had served God's purpose in his own generation, he fell asleep. This event did not take God by surprise. He was very present in that ICU room, welcoming my sweetheart into His eternal kingdom. Bill did not go home one second before God called him, or one second later. He had served his Lord to the best of his ability, and it was time.

God's ways and His timing are often in conflict with our timing and desires. This was not my timing. Bill and I had unfulfilled plans for our future together. We had hopes and dreams that we often talked about. Growing old together sounded wonderful to both of us. We have a sign in our bedroom and also in our yard in Murrells Inlet that reads, "Grow old with me, the best is yet to be," which was written by Robert Browning. My first thought when I read that sign after November 1, 2017, was, "Well, I guess that didn't happen!"

My heart and mind changed a few days later when the Lord showed me a new and better meaning for that familiar quote. We indeed *had* grown old together. Bill was seventy-three, and I was seventy-two, and we had been married for fifty-four years. Yes, we had grown old together. And guess what? The best for both of us is indeed yet to be. Heaven will be infinitely better than life here on earth. Bill has now seen his Redeemer and tasted of heaven's magnificence. I look forward to when my time comes. But first, I have to serve all the purposes that God has in His heart for me before He will call me home.

I think writing this book is one of His purposes for me.

REMINDERS

Bill and I loved praise music. We played it often as we allowed the words of Scripture to penetrate our hearts. But next in line for music greatness, there was no disagreement between us. Definitely we chose the oldies! We weren't great dancers, but we surely loved our rock 'n' roll songs. Although we were high school sweethearts, we didn't dance much early on, but as the years passed, we discovered that we both really enjoyed recapturing our youth by dancing.

We danced in Riviera Maya, we boogied at weddings, but we enjoyed letting loose in our living room most often. From "Old Time Rock and Roll" to "Unchained Melody" to "Twilight Time," we practiced our cool steps where no one else could judge or critique. We talked about taking ballroom dancing lessons but never made the time or commitment to do so. I wish we had.

Bill took many of our favorite songs and made a playlist and then created CDs for us to enjoy in our car while traveling or put them on his MP3 player to use at the gym. I never learned to operate the player with earbuds while exercising, but I did enjoy our car rides. I can still hear him singing our love songs. Neither Bill nor I had great voices, especially him, but for me, there was nothing quite so wonderful as hearing him sing to me with his whole heart, even if off-key.

When you lose someone, reminders seem to appear out of nowhere and can take your breath away. The first time I turned on the CD player in my car after Bill went to heaven, his playlist filled the air. At first, it was too emotional and brought tears for me to hear our songs. In a short while, I found that listening to melodies that had meaning for us as a couple caused another inch of healing in that mile-long journey of grief. I would turn off the news or the latest hits on the radio and elect to listen to Bill's playlist. As I cleaned out the center console, I discovered he had several different CDs, and now I rotate them in my car player. I may wear them out.

As I write this entry, it has been two years and four months since Bill changed his address. I still find cheater eyeglasses in odd places. Bill never was comfortable wearing glasses even though he increasingly needed them. He found that cheaters worked well, so he owned many pairs and stored them wherever he might find himself—at his workbench, in the car, at his desk, or in the TV room.

He used the same plan for the bent-paperclip toothpick. I know, not a good thing for dental hygiene, but he had a space in the back of his teeth that stored food after meals. No other type of toothpick worked, so he repurposed his own. How my heart skips when I find one of these tools in a dresser drawer or nightstand.

Mostly, I enjoy finding little love notes that he sent me and that I saved. For that reason alone, I am grateful to be somewhat of a pack rat. I have files, and I store a lot of stuff.

We often wrote each other notes. I would put mine in his shaving drawer or under his pillow or in his lunch bag. My favorite note from him is on a faded yellow Post-It Note, and it says, "Do I ever love you!"

Oh my!

DAFFODILS WILL BLOOM AGAIN

As I said in the introduction, the Lord showed me I also have a race to run. I can't just roll up in a ball and cower in the corner in this new season of life. At first, I felt purposeless, alone, and numb. In his book *The Disciple-Making Church*, Glenn McDonald shares a similar story on page 141 about Lyman Coleman, the founder of Serendipity Small Group Resources. Lyman lost his wife, Margaret, in the fall of 2000 and shared his reflections during his grieving process. He had a caring neighbor say to him, "You're going to make a choice in six months to live or die."

Lyman chose to live. He said that with money people gave for a memorial to Margaret, he purchased daffodil bulbs and gave them to neighbors and friends to plant in her memory. Lyman talked about the daffodils in this quote:

> It has been a cold winter and the daffodils are still underground, but in a little while they will bloom in all their glory. It has been a long winter for me, too. I feel like I don't belong anywhere. To anyone. I am lonely. Lost. But Easter is coming. We will be together

again. Jesus promised it. I believe it. The daffodils will bloom again.

Because Jesus lives, Lyman chose to live also. Jesus not only lives, but He is also Lord of the universe and the Savior of those who put their trust in Him. Christ follower Margaret Coleman is also alive, and Christ follower Bill Blacksmith lives as well across the veil. Each person who looks to Jesus Christ and surrenders their life to Him is promised eternal life. The winter of grief can be long, cold, and lonely. But the daffodils will bloom again, and Easter is coming.

I try not to be weird about it, but I really don't like to refer to Bill as dead, passed on, or gone. I don't even think of him that way. Bill is more alive today than he has ever been. That gives me great comfort, and it also gives me great impetus to keep putting one foot in front of the other and to get up in the morning. The Lord sits on the throne, and He has my life under control, and my future is secure in His able Hands. He wants me to continue to surrender my life to Him, even though imperfectly, and to trust Him all along the way, even as I walk through the shadow of death. He has a plan, and with the Holy Spirit empowering me, I will successfully finish out this life and be one day with Him.

Lord, how I long for Your presence.

REMEMBERING A LEGACY

Bill and I had often talked about end-of-life issues. I am so glad we did. I think our age had something to do with that conversation, but so did his kidney transplant. When you know that God has extended your life, you recognize what a gift it is and how fragile it is. We were very grateful for the days that the Lord gave us both. Our love story was enhanced also by the realization that God was in charge of our life and our days. We valued our time together.

One thing I never thought to discuss with Bill was how we wanted to remember each other after we passed. What would our legacy look like? I know our lives belong to God and He will leave any legacy He desires us to have, but I wanted to remember Bill's life by something tangible.

Since he loved wrestling and was an alumnus of Lock Haven University, I thought it would be fitting to establish a small scholarship to honor him. It would help a wrestler pursuing health and physical education to offset some of his expenses. We were also committed to helping provide clean water in third-world countries, so there is now a plaque on a couple of wells somewhere in this world in honor of Reverend Dr. Bill Blacksmith. The people that are served by these wells will never know Bill, but I feel comforted in knowing that his name is written there.

In lieu of flowers at his celebration of life, I decided that I wanted friends and family to donate toward the life group ministry at our church. Bill's heart was turned toward anything that would help people grow in their relationship with Jesus. At Graystone Church, we established a life group resource section of the church library where donations were used to buy kits of DVDs, books, and study guide resources. A lovely plaque with Bill's picture and biography marks the spot along the dark wood bookshelves in that two-hundred-year-old building.

We've all seen races where an athlete runs around a track and passes a baton to the next team member. In essence, when one has passed the baton, their race is over and the one receiving it must now run. Bill and I wanted to give our family some sort of baton to illustrate our commissioning them to run their race with Jesus as we were nearing the end of our race. It would soon be their turn. We had not as yet made the baton gifts a reality. After the end of Bill's race, I decided that the time had come to make it happen.

You can find almost anything on Amazon, and I looked for batons. After eliminating the category of those that majorettes twirl, I came upon the batons that track runners pass in relays. I was able to purchase a silver-colored twelve-inch-long tube made of metal. It was perfect. A friend, Valerie, scrawled beautiful calligraphy on each, saying, "I have fought the good fight, I have finished the race, I have kept the faith." This is the scripture found in 2 Timothy 4:7–8 (NIV) that we used in Bill's celebration of life. At Thanksgiving, I success-fully passed the baton to the next generation, charging them to run their race well.

In these small ways I memorialized Bill's legacy. A name can be written on a headstone, on a water well sign, on a schol-arship letter, on a plaque in a library, or on a baton, but the only place that a written name is eternally important is if it is written in the Lamb's Book of Life. God wrote Bill's name there September 5, 1971, when he received the gift of eternal life by accepting Jesus' sacrifice on the cross for his sin.

OIL CHANGES AND
PHYSICAL THERAPY

Over the years, we only purchased one car that was brand-new. I think it was the little green Volkswagen that we drove until the floor started to fall out. We gave it away when it became evident that we might lose one of the children! All the other cars we owned were preowned. We used to call them used cars, but *preowned* sounds so much nicer. Someone told us that buying a used car was a financially wise move. If you buy a new car, you lose money as soon as you drive it off the lot. With a used car, the bulk of depreciation has already occurred. Whatever way you slice it, Bill and I were committed to saving by driving preowned cars. We also saved to buy our cars with cash. That was hard to do sometimes, but we decided it was the right way to go for our family.

By choosing this route of buying preowned, we knew that sooner or later we would be making repairs. Car parts do eventually wear out. Our three- to five-thousand-mile oil changes, we made mandatory. Rotation of our tires was important when needed. At those yearly inspections, our car guy knew to look over everything and fix what was questionable. We often chuckled that we knew our mechanic's phone number by heart.

This isn't a deeply significant memory except that it reminds me of my body as I age. I have had arthritis in my knees for quite a long time, and an MRI recently discovered tears in various parts of my shoulder.

I am falling apart, I have thought. *I don't want to spend all this time at the doctor's office, and I am weary of going to physical therapy.*

I have a friend, Barbara, who is a writer and also a life coach. On occasion I have met with her to ask writing questions or get her take on how I am doing in my journey of life without Bill. I was sharing with her about how much time maintenance on my physical body is taking and that I am feeling weary of all the doctor appointments and physical therapy sessions. She put all my concerns in perspective by asking me what my priorities of life were right now. I said that I wanted to write this book, spend time with my family, serve by teaching my life group, and minister any other way the Lord wanted. She reminded me of a theological concept that I had forgotten. As a Christian, my body, Scripture says, is the temple of the Holy Spirit. I need to care for that temple. If I want to be able to do all the things on my bucket list, I need a healthy body to accomplish them.

Whew! That is a game changer! Yes, if my body isn't as good as it can be at my age, then everything else goes downhill. The doctor visits, the shots in my knees and shoulders, the walking I try to do, the water I drink, and the food I eat are all sort of like the oil changes and tire rotations in my car. Body parts do age and wear out. It was such a wonderful reminder of that fact and of the fact that I need to pay attention to my body, even more so now that I am older. If I am going to finish my race strong, then I need to do my part. I can trust God with the rest.

Yes, and I even know God's phone number by heart.

BRING FORTH THE ROYAL DIADEM

It would soon be my turn to take the stage and stand behind the podium to receive Bill's award. Nearly two years had passed since he went to heaven, and his alma mater, Lock Haven University, awarded him a place in the newly established Athletic Hall of Fame. I wanted to do a good job with my speech, and I was thrilled that the Lord had given me ideas in my sleep one night. I walked with wobbly knees up the steps to the stage.

"Thank you and good afternoon to all the Lock Haven Athletic fans here today. It is my great pleasure to accept this Lock Haven Athletic Hall of Fame honor for my husband, Bill Blacksmith.

"There are many things I could tell you about Bill. He loved life, and he loved adventure. He was a wonderful husband and father, and he loved me and his kids and grandkids. He had compiled a list called 'seventy-two things to do at Grami and Papa's house.' He really did love his grandkids and enjoyed every minute he had with them. He was purposeful about how he lived his life. He was good at just about any physical endeavor that he tried, but wrestling was his passion. When he entered Cedar Cliff High School, the only wrestling with which he was familiar was professional wrestling with Bobo Brazil and Bruno San Martino. He told me he was so disappointed when he walked into the gym on his first day of wrestling practice and couldn't see any ropes! (Yes, that was a joke! Bill said I couldn't tell a joke worth a darn. I am so glad you laughed). He soon got the hang of things, and under the excellent tutelage of Coach Bob Craig, he became a good high school wrestler.

"Bill attended Lock Haven from 1962 to 1966, and as far as I remember, it was the only college he ever wanted to attend. Coach Craig, a five-sport athlete, graduated from Lock Haven in 1953. Bob was Bill's hero, and Bill's plan was to attend Lock Haven, wrestle, and then return to the Harrisburg area to coach wrestling at Cedar Cliff High School. He had hoped to take over when Bob retired. God had other plans.

"At Lock Haven, Bill was blessed to have teammates that pushed him to excel, like Fred, Jerry, Biff, Ken, and Dick, to name a few, and to have a wonderful coach like Gray Simons. He loved to tell his children and grandchildren old wrestling stories, and they even got to meet Gray at this year's NCAA tournament. It was quite a thrill.

"Bill was a fighter and a tough competitor. Bill's 'tight waist' and 'sit out' were legendary. He served as head wrestling coach at Indiana University of Pennsylvania for seventeen years, and in retirement he worked with kids on the wrestling mat at two local high schools. He fought against kidney disease when he was thirty and received a kidney transplant when he was fifty-two. He never—and I mean never—let anything get in the way of doing life. He worked hard, he played hard, and he even suited up with protection pads and played ice hockey when he was using peritoneal dialysis. Life was an adventure, and he lived it to the fullest.

"He attended school for twelve years from first grade through high school and majored in sports, social events, and girls. So he always said the Lord gave him twelve more years to apply himself and do better. He did indeed do better the second twelve. He finished college, his master's degree, his doctorate degree, and then seminary. Bill was a full professor at IUP for his career and taught in the undergraduate and graduate schools. He was a sport psychologist.

"In 1966, after Bill won the Division I NCAA title in the 145-pound class, *The Patriot-News* in Harrisburg ran an article on the sports page that said, 'Blacksmith wins National Diadem.' A *diadem* isn't a word we use much, if at all, in our vocabulary, but we discovered it is a 'crown for the victor.'

"Fast-forward to 1971, when Bill became a Christian. Over the next years he became a softer and gentler version of that cocky young wrestler who won the NCAA diadem. He began to attend church. One of the old hymns we sang was called 'All Hail the Power of Jesus' Name' and it had this phrase, 'Bring forth the royal diadem and crown Him Lord of all.' There was that word, *diadem*. Bill looked up that article that we had saved among all the other wrestling memorabilia and recalled how excited, proud, and overjoyed he was when he won that crown, that diadem, in 1966. But nothing—and I mean nothing—compared with the excitement he experienced when he gave his life to Jesus Christ and began to walk with Him.

"Bill was a faithful follower and became a competent Bible teacher. He heard the call of God when he was in his forties and attended seminary and retired early to serve his first church when he was sixty. In the celebration of life we had after Bill went to heaven on November 1, 2017, we used a scripture from the Bible that says, 'I have fought the good fight, I have finished the race, I have kept the faith. Now there is in store for me the crown of righteousness which the Lord, the Righteous Judge will award to me on that day—and not only for me but also to all who have longed for His appearing' (2 Tim. 4:7–8 NIV).

"Bill won a diadem many times for his wrestling prowess, but at the end of life he received a crown that will not fade or tarnish that Jesus won for him on Calvary, a forever crown.

"Lock Haven University, I thank you so very much for this honor today, and I receive it with gratitude for my wonderful husband, Bill Blacksmith."

GOD'S NUDGES

So often in this book-writing process, I have felt God's nudges. Google says that *nudge* is to "prod gently, particularly with one's elbow, to draw attention to something." Bill and I would often elbow each other during a teaching or sermon when we wanted the other to catch the speaker's point. Bill called that gesture the elbow of God. God's elbow has taken on various other forms for me now. Sometimes it is a thought or feeling, and often it happens in the night or as I am waking in the morning. I am learning the importance of keeping a tablet at my bedside so I can write down the "nudge" because I am prone to forget.

I had been asking my Father just how to finish this book. Last night or early this morning, I was given the idea of ending with a prayer. Sounds good to me.

*****

Heavenly Father, I am grateful for this opportunity to write about You. I really could have filled many more pages with accounts of Your blessings, teachings, and corrections that I have felt in my life over the years, but these are the reflections I have chosen. You are a mighty God and a loving Father. Thank You.

I am grateful to be able to reflect on the many, many memories of Bill that continually flow through my mind and heart. Our love story was unique, and I am grateful. He was not in my life by accident. You are sovereign, and You brought us together, and it was a wild and wonderful journey. I learned from him, and he learned from me. You worked in both of us to accomplish Your plan for our lives. You mend broken vessels, and You mold the clay of lives into what You choose. This particular vessel is grateful.

It was an awesome discipline of looking back at the years past and the life You gave us to live. I see Your hand of provision, protection, guidance, and forgiveness in it all. Our world is broken, and as an individual, I am broken, but You are at work to make my paths straight and level and my mountains low. You are healing my broken heart.

Lord, if the reader of this book is a believer in Jesus Christ, please use this saga to encourage him or her to continue to "fight the good fight and run their race." May they be nudged to affect their world for Your good and for Your glory. If my reader does not yet know the saving grace of Jesus Christ, I pray You will draw his or her heart to You. Jesus is the Way, the Truth, and the Life, and no one comes to You except through Him. May they grow to know that truth.

My heart's desire through this book, whether read by few or many, is to bring glory to You, Father, for You are worthy. I also want to honor my husband, for he was the most dedicated Christ follower I know, and I believe he is now standing in Your presence, enjoying all the great benefits of life forever with You. I want to share my life experiences to encourage others along this journey. Life is hard, and I want my life to witness to Your grace and goodness.

To God be the glory. In Jesus' name. Amen.

CPSIA information can be obtained
at www.ICGtesting.com
Printed in the USA
LVHW080830290920
667382LV00021B/3024